"I celebrate Martha Zimmerman's *Celebrating Biblical Feasts* as a feast of its own. Loaded with insights and background, and full of wonderfully practical ideas, this book will be an important tool for all who seek to bring the Bible into 21st century life. Parents, homeschoolers, Christian educators, and pastors will all find an abundance of ideas to help develop an awareness of the rhythms of life through participation in re-enactments of the biblical feasts. I loved this book in its earlier edition; I rejoice that it is being made available in this new and updated edition for another generation of parents and teachers."

> —Maxine Hancock, Ph.D.
> Author, *Living on Less & Liking it More, Re-evaluating Your Commitments*
> Professor of Interdisciplinary Studies and Spiritual Theology
> Regent College, Vancouver, B.C.

"Why should we Jews have all the fun? This book shows Christians how to incorporate the joy, wisdom and human interrelating of biblical celebrations into their family and communal life. I say 'family and communal life' rather than just 'life' because this book, unlike much of Western Christianity, does not emphasize primarily the individual. Martha Zimmerman has absorbed the Jewish—and biblical—emphasis on community and family, and she teaches it to all who will read her engaging book. By celebrating these festivals Christians will not be 'Judaizing' themselves but enriching their lives and enhancing their experience of the Lord. So join with the Lord, join with the Jewish people, and join in the fun."

> —David H. Stern, Ph.D.
> Translator, *Jewish New Testament* and the *Complete Jewish Bible*
> Author, *Jewish New Testament Commentary, Messianic Jewish Manifesto*, and *Restoring the Jewishness of the Gospel: A Message for Christians*

"Martha Zimmerman's book has been a treasury of inspiration on a much-neglected aspect of Scripture. It has amazing appeal in cultures where people want to comprehend God with their entire being. When I use the teaching of the biblical feasts in Africa, tribal people invariably respond: 'We had heard, but now we have seen, felt, smelled, and tasted how wonderful our God is.'"

> —Peter Wiegand
> Torchbearers Austria

Celebrating
Biblical Feasts
In Your Home or Church

Martha Zimmerman

BETHANYHOUSE
Minneapolis, Minnesota

Celebrating Biblical Feasts
Copyright © 1981, 2004
Martha Zimmerman

Cover design by Danielle White

Page 191 is a continuation of the copyright page.

Originally published as *Celebrate the Feasts*

Published by Bethany House Publishers
11400 Hampshire Avenue South
Bloomington, Minnesota 55438
www.bethanyhouse.com

Bethany House Publishers is a Division of
Baker Book House Company, Grand Rapids, Michigan.

Printed in the United States of America

Library of Congress Cataloging-in-Publication Data

Zimmerman, Martha, 1934–
   [Celebrate the feasts of the Old Testament in your own home or church]

   Celebrating biblical feasts in your home or church / by Martha Zimmerman.
      p. cm.
Orginally published: Celebrate the feasts of the Old Testament in your own home or church. Minneapolis, Minn. : Bethany Fellowship, c1981.
   ISBN 0-7642-2897-8 (pbk.)
   1. Family—Religious life. 2. Worship programs. 3. Fasts and feasts in the Bible.
I. Title.
   BV4526.3.Z56   2004
   249—dc22   2003023569

This book was written to honor my parents,
MARGARET and DICK GADSKE.
It has been
taught with love and diligence to our children—
JOHN, RICHARD, and SARAH.

About the Author

Martha Zimmerman was taught to love Jewish people and their celebrations as a child. She and her husband passed along this tradition to their three now-adult children. An adjunct faculty member at Carey Theological College in Vancouver, British Columbia, Martha is a frequent speaker at churches and conferences and a guest on radio talk shows throughout North America. She and her husband make their home in Washington. She is the author of *Celebrating Biblical Feasts* and *Celebrating the Christian Year*.

Foreword

I welcome the republication of *Celebrating Biblical Feasts* by Martha Zimmerman.

We Christians owe a great deal to our Jewish heritage. In the early church a fierce battle was waged against the Gnostics who repudiated the Jews, their faith and worship. But the Fathers of the church were right in insisting that Hebrew faith and Christian truth were continuous.

Using the pictures of Christ in the Old Testament, early interpreters of the faith saw that all the events, offices, and feasts of Hebrew faith found their fulfillment in Jesus Christ. Today the study of the feasts of Israel will lead Christians to a greater appreciation and deeper devotion to Jesus who is the fulfillment of them all.

Also, the practice of a rhythm of time that shapes and forms the spiritual life is a great contribution of Israel. Following in their footsteps Christians mark time with the fulfillment of all of Israel's feasts in the incarnation, the death and resurrection of Jesus, and the coming of the Holy Spirit.

Read *Celebrating Biblical Feasts* and see Jesus, the incarnate Son of God, redeemer of the world.

Robert Webber
Myers Professor of Ministry
Northern Baptist Theological Seminary
Lombard, Illinois

Preface

"Hey, Mom! You're right! Habakkuk *is* in the Bible."

Sure that I was hearing things, I called back to our twelve-year-old son, "What did you say?" His response was a surprise.

"Well, the other day I heard you talking about some book in the Bible called Habakkuk, and I just found it."

My response still shocks me; the words are burned into my memory! "Richard, haven't 'they' taught you the books of the Bible yet in Sunday school?"

God prepares us in amazing ways for His new lessons. His timing is perfect. I had just finished writing a paper for one of my seminary courses on Deuteronomy 6:1–9 which says, "And you shall love the Lord your God with all your heart, and with all your soul, and with all your might. And these words which I am commanding you today shall be on your heart, and *you* shall teach them diligently to your children. . . ." I knew it didn't say "Sunday school teachers" or "fellowship leaders" or "the great staff at our church" (all of those people are glad to help)—but the command is to parents. *You* shall teach them. If God gives us something to do, He will enable us to do it!

At that moment I didn't know where the next step would take us; but I knew from experience that when His instructions are followed, the end for which they are given will be accomplished. The results are God's business. He was calling *me* to be faithful.

Many questions followed, such as: How? When? Are you sure?—Me, God? We talked about it as a family. The children's suggestions were helpful and encouraging. It was obvious they were eager and ready to begin a new adventure.

When I started looking for materials to teach "Christian Education in the Home," my search led to the best possible source! Since God said "do it" in the Bible, I reasoned the Bible would tell us what to do. And it did!

This book has been growing ever since. We have learned a lot, known God's blessing, and had many fun and funny times together! We want to share our adventures, not as a model to copy but as guidelines to encourage you in creatively teaching the marvelous truths of the Old Testament with New Testament understanding.

I want to thank Homer Goddard, whose vision brought Fuller Seminary Extension to Richland, Washington; David Stoop, adjunct professor of the seminary class on Creative Teaching, who encouraged me to write this book; Judy Moy, Christian Education Director, who met with me once a week to pray and share; the William Markillie family and the Roger Johnson family, who spent three years celebrating these festivals with us, giving their support; many friends who joined us and shared in prayer; Sharynn Freiheit, who found helpful ways to care for our family; Terry Sullivan for technical support; Joanne Fankhauser, Betty Phillips, and Sally Rossello, who did all of the typing; John, John Jr., Richard, and Sarah for suggestions and constant encouragement. I want to thank the many churches who have taken up the challenge to prepare parents for their God appointed task.

Habakkuk *is* in the Bible. So is Leviticus. Chapter 23 is where we started. It was our outline for the family times presented on the following pages.

Martha Zimmerman
Blaine, Washington

Contents

Chapter 5: Rosh Hashanah

A Day of Blowing

What is Rosh Hashanah? What is Tashlich? Why is the ram's horn significant? Apples dipped in honey and other symbolic foods. A time of preparation.

Chapter 6: Yom Kippur

A Day of Returning

What is Yom Kippur? Biblical basis. Fasting and feasting. Blessing the children. Putting things in order.

Chapter 7: Sukkoth

A Family Fort Festival

What is Sukkoth? Simhat Torah? Directions for building a Sukkah. Children learn what they live.

And beginning with Moses and with all the prophets,
He [Jesus] explained to them the things concerning
Himself in all the Scriptures.
(Luke 24:27)

Introduction

Beginning an Adventure

Puzzles are a challenge. They are also lots of fun. It always feels good to find a piece that fits. Having found one, you want to find "one more." When my dad began to work a jigsaw puzzle, he located all the border pieces first. Jesus is like the frame or border around the entire Bible. His life draws all the pieces together. One of the miracles of God's Word is that all the pieces fit! Every person, place, event, and story adds to the completed picture. The Old and New Testaments belong *together!* Once you understand and believe that Jesus is central to *all* truth ("I am . . . the truth"—John 14:6), even some odd shapes fit.

An essential border piece, Matthew 1:1, reminds us that Jesus was Jewish: "The book of the genealogy of Jesus Christ the son of David, the son of Abraham." Some other border pieces are bits of evidence found throughout the Gospels: He obeyed God's commandments, celebrated each biblical feast, and regarded all of the festivals as ordained by God to be remembered, observed, and celebrated. He said, "Don't misunderstand why I have come—it isn't to cancel the laws of Moses and the warnings of the prophets." (Don't throw away half of the puzzle pieces and expect a finished picture when you are through.) "I came to fulfill them, and to make them all come true" (fit together). *"Those who teach* God's laws and obey them shall be great in the Kingdom of Heaven" (Matt. 5:17, 19, TLB).

This book contains suggestions for celebrating the biblical festivals. I believe that they are key puzzle pieces. Paul had something to say to us about them: "Some think that Christians should observe the Jewish holidays as special days to worship God, but others say it is wrong and foolish to go to all that trouble, for every day alike belongs to God. On questions of this kind everyone must decide for himself. If you have special days for worshipping the Lord, you are trying to honor him; you are doing a good thing" (Rom. 14:5–6, TLB). The suggestions presented here for celebrating the feasts are not to be a legalistic set of rules to earn God's favor but are to be used as teaching tools to help our families honor God.

Let's go back in time. A very large puzzle piece tucked in Deuteronomy is called the Great Shema. Just as the Israelites were about to enter the Promised Land, Moses encouraged Israel to love God with all their hearts. To impress them with a deep sense of their need for God and to prepare them for the inheritance which He had planned for them, this commandment is presented in a positive form: "And you shall love the Lord your God. . . ." The following is the text of Deuteronomy 6:1–9 (TLB):

> The Lord your God told me to give you all these commandments which you are to obey in the land you will soon be entering, where you will live. The purpose of these laws is to cause you, your sons, and your grandsons to reverence the Lord your God by obeying all of his instructions as long as you live; if you do, you will have long, prosperous years ahead of you. Therefore, O Israel, listen closely to each command and be careful to obey it, so that all will go well with you, and so that you will have many children. If you obey these commands you will become a great nation in a glorious land "flowing with milk and honey," even as the God of your fathers promised you.
>
> O Israel, listen: Jehovah is our God, Jehovah alone. You

must love him with *all* your heart, soul and might. And you must think constantly about these commandments I am giving you today. You must teach them to your children and talk about them when you are at home or out for a walk; at bedtime and the first thing in the morning. Tie them on your finger, wear them on your forehead, and write them on the door-posts of your house!

God's Word is life. It is His gift. We are challenged to affirm life, know the blessing of God, and live long in the abundance of His love. Jesus said, "I am come that they might have life, and that they might have it more abundantly" (John 10:10, KJV).

The message is urgent: Hear, therefore, O Israel, nation that sprang from Jacob, and be careful to do this. People, you really should listen. . . . God is to be heard! Give this your careful attention. *If it is performed, the purpose for which it was given will be accomplished.*

The Lord God is a personal God. He is to be *loved.* The word for "love" in this passage is from the vocabulary of family life. Love of God is what life is all about. Love draws us to obedience. Obedience to His Word is the demonstration of your love toward Him, and this loving response to the Lord's great goodness requires giving of yourself to Him. Open your heart to the living voice of the Divine Teacher.

In Hebrew, the name for the first five books of the Bible is Torah. It means guidance, direction, instruction, and information. Job 36:22 asks, "Who is a teacher like Him?" With the Psalmist we should say, "Teach me your way" (Ps. 27:11, NIV).

Both the Old and New Testaments present the same principle: "Teach them to your children. Talk about them . . ." (Deut. 11:19, TLB); "And, fathers, . . . bring them up in the discipline and instruction of the Lord" (Eph. 6:4). We as parents need to hear this. The utmost care must be given to help our children understand. The more they *understand,* the more they will *believe.*

I call this the principle of familiar things. Remember how you feel when the picture of a place you have visited flashes on your TV screen? Familiar things feel good! The word "teach" in the Deuteronomy passage means repeat and re-repeat the instructions. Excite their attention! Stimulate their interest. The Word of God is to be kept before their eyes.

But how? The following verbs could be found on a current list of good teaching techniques: experience, talk, write, and use visual aids. The adverbs in the scripture passage suggest constantly and diligently. Later, Paul said "gently." The Living Bible puts it this way, "Talk about them when you are at home or out for a walk; at bedtime and the first thing in the morning." There is no better method than this. You should begin and end the day with the Lord. Include Him in your everyday living and, therefore, with *awareness* talk, walk, lie down, get up, always knowing God's presence wherever you are. The atmosphere of your home should be saturated with the Lord's presence.

God's words are to be more than just heard or read; they are to be an affair of the heart. Jeremiah 31:33 says, "I will put My law within them, and on their heart I will write it." If God's Word "dwells in your heart," you will be anxious to teach it to your children. It is your faith and duty. The word "remember" is repeated in the Old and New Testaments over 300 times. Phrases such as "remember the deeds of the Lord," "remember His marvelous works," "do this in remembrance," are familiar. First Samuel 12:24 says, "Consider what great things He has done for you."

The challenge is: How do we relate the past to the present? How do we actively "consider" and "remember"? Our children love to look at their baby books. Pictures from birthday parties and special events in their lives help us to remember these special times. An old proverb says, "Put something where you can see it so your eye will remind your heart."

Reading the great stories in the Bible, the accounts of God's amazing love, provision and protection, is a good, steady first step. But *celebrating* Hebrew traditions recorded in the Bible provides visual reminders and encourages awareness of the Lord's presence and His blessings. Biblical festivals are living experiences.

This should help you "feel" the difference. Imagine a typical Sunday school class. The teacher sits in a circle with her children. She points to a visual aid as she tells the story of Abraham and his descendants. Now contrast this scene with a living experience. Lately we have been having grey, overcast days. Last night the weather changed and the fog lifted. The stars seemed especially bright and Sarah noticed them with delight. It was the right time to pick up the flashlight and Bible and go outside under the stars. There we *read* the story of Abraham in Genesis 15:5, *looked* up at the heavens, tried to *count* the stars, and *talked* about God's unique family of people who have multiplied and survived down through the generations.

Too often we try to relegate God to a "time" period. One hour a week in Sunday school is not enough. My goal is to help you create a learning situation in your home that is constant, natural, and meaningful. If your child sees, hears, smells, tastes, and feels the Word of God, profound impressions will be made on that young life!

Celebrate and remember the deeds of the Lord as a family. Children learn what they live!

"And the Word became flesh, and dwelt among us" (John 1:14).

Therefore the Lord blessed the sabbath
day and made it holy.
(Exodus 20:11)

Chapter 1

Sabbath

A Weekend Celebration for the Family

What Is Sabbath?

The Lord spoke to Moses, saying, "Speak to the sons of Israel, and say to them, 'The Lord's appointed times . . . are these.'" Following this text of Leviticus, chapter twenty-three, God's first appointment with us is for Sabbath. It's "Number One" on His list of holy days, both in its listing and frequency.

Sabbath comes from the Hebrew word *Shabbat,* meaning "rest." It was born in the very beginning: "Thus the heavens and the earth were finished . . . and He rested. . . . God blessed the seventh day, and sanctified it: because in it he had rested from all his work which God created and made" (Gen. 2:1–3, KJV). The Sabbath was instituted as a memorial to His creation. This memorial is so important that it was included in the

Ten Commandments given by God to His people on Mount Sinai: *"Remember* the sabbath day, to keep it holy. Six days you shall labor and do all your work, but the seventh day is a sabbath of the Lord your God; in it you shall not do any work, you or your son or your daughter . . . or your sojourner who stays with you. For in six days the Lord made the heavens and the earth, the sea and all that is in them, and rested on the seventh day; therefore the Lord blessed the sabbath day and made it holy" (Ex. 20:8–11). And in Deuteronomy 5:12, *"Observe* the sabbath day to keep it holy. . . ."

These two words, remember and observe, help us understand how we are to approach and live out this day. "Remember" suggests inward thoughts of love and devotion. But that isn't enough. "Observe" becomes the expression of our feelings. Sabbath combines love and law, devotion and obedience, feelings and observances.

Hebrew tradition tells us that as God presented the commandments, He spoke to Moses and said, "I have a precious gift stored away in my treasures and its name is Sabbath. I desire to give this gift to Israel. Go and inform them of it."

We so often miss what God intends for our good. It wasn't long before the day that God had planned for our good became filled with "thou shalt nots," almost to the exclusion of recreation. An early prophet reminded Israel to observe the Sabbath as a delight, not a burden. Jesus taught, "The Sabbath was made for man, and not man for the Sabbath" (Mark 2:27). "I desire compassion, and not a sacrifice . . ." (Matt. 12:7). "It is right to do good on the Sabbath" (Matt. 12:12, TLB).

The actions of Jesus were misunderstood on various occasions. He was distressed with the misguided teachings of the religious leaders in reference to Sabbath—*not* with the Sabbath itself. He loved and observed Sabbath. In fact, He declared Himself to be the Lord of the Sabbath. His life demonstrated compassion, mercy, and loving respect for God and His creation, not mere rules and regulations.

The Pharisees took the commandment "to rest" and carried it to a ridiculous end which distorted God's original purpose. In our day, some overreact against Sabbath restrictions, tending to neglect or forget the importance of the day and giving it only a token place in their lives.

So much of life as we know it has become hectic and exhausting. Important meetings, exciting activities, sports events and very good causes are pulling families in a thousand different ways. People everywhere are busy being busy—never stopping to *really* rest.

When balanced, our activities during the week become preparation time for the Sabbath, somewhat like a path leading us to the gate of a garden. Sabbath was a gift of time in which to put things in order and allow God to be God in our lives. It can become a time for us to rediscover places inside ourselves that are forgotten during the rest of the busy week. No wonder the week pivots around this special day. A simple diagram lets us see the progression.

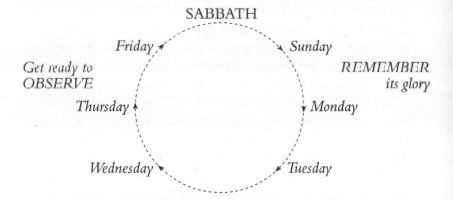

SABBATH

Friday → ← Sunday

Get ready to
OBSERVE

REMEMBER
its glory

Thursday ↑ ↓ Monday

Wednesday ← ← Tuesday

This is to be a day filled with special joy that draws the family together. Phrases like "hurry up" or "I'm too busy" have no place, as we give the gift of time to each other. Our attitude, whatever it is, toward the Sabbath will be contagious. In the recovery of this biblical tradition, we have the privilege of ushering peace into our home. It is our responsibility to celebrate and preserve it.

Sabbath Friday

"And it was the Preparation Day, and the Sabbath was about to begin" (Luke 23:54).

What you will need:

1. pair of candle holders
2. two white candles (with matches close by)
3. cup of wine or grape juice
4. bowl of water and a towel
5. two loaves of braided bread (or two rolls)
6. napkin
7. Bible
8. special dinner

How to celebrate!

There is a lot to do, but with care and planning these activities, too, will be part of the celebration. A checklist on page 47 will help you to organize. The house should be cleaned, special foods prepared, the table set (with your best), candles and matches in place. This probably sounds like normal preparations for "company." Think of what these actions will say to your family since they are the ones who are being honored with this attention. I know it made an impression on my family. Questions like "Who's coming over tonight?" "You're doing this for *us?*" made me know it was worth the effort. Let everyone help! Part of the purpose is for the family to be together. If everyone joins in, all of the work will get done and everyone can enjoy the rest.

At our house, it is customary to pick a flower for the Sabbath table, or bring in some beautiful fall leaves, depending on the season. This is a time to put away artificial centerpieces and bring in something special from God's creation.

The mood of the evening is gentle and quiet. Peace has come at last to the home. Never confuse this with long faces and formality. Approach the table at which this meal is served as if it is an altar, knowing that we can always meet God and receive His blessing with joy and personal friendship. This table should be a place where we can enjoy God's presence while having a good time together. "There you shall eat in the presence of the Lord your God and rejoice, you and your household" (Deut. 14:26b).

Just before the sun goes down the family gathers. A parent (traditionally the mother) begins the evening with prayer. (See pages 36–41 for the details of this special supper pageant.) As the sun slips away she recites a special blessing and lights the Sabbath candles. She may pray silently for her children, that they will grow up with hearts open to understand and appreciate God's Word. Each child receives a blessing from a parent (traditionally the father). Couples will enjoy this place in the service where the husband honors his wife by reading from Proverbs 31. Softly the family sings a blessing to each other. These blessings produced all kinds of emotions in us, a little embarrassed at first, but very special. After everyone is seated, a parent (traditionally the father) recites the Kiddush, a Sabbath prayer over the wine, and passes the cup for all to sip and enjoy. (If you are uncomfortable with the use of actual wine, small individual glasses of grape juice may be set at each place.) A bowl of water is provided for washing hands. Hamotzi, the blessing of the bread, is next. Now the meal is served, LEISURELY. The grace after the meal should never be forgotten.

"And on the Sabbath they rested according to the commandment" (Luke 23:56). Enjoy this evening. All that is left to do is rest. A delightful little children's book, *The Jewish Sabbath,* puts it this way: "Some people rest by closing their eyes and thinking. Some people rest by walking or visiting, or reading, or playing. Rest means being free to just be. A person is a person on the Sabbath."* Be assured, "The Lord will give strength to His people; the Lord will bless His people with peace" (Ps. 29:11).

Sabbath Symbols and Their Meaning

Candles: In ancient times, before clocks and modern-day communication systems, a blast from the shofar, a ram's horn, signaled the people of Israel to stop working and begin to observe the Sabbath. Just before the sun went down, lamps were lit in homes to shine through the dusk and evening hours. The tradition of lighting candles has continued. The mother of the family lights the Sabbath candles. She does this because Eve, the first mother, extinguished the light of eternal life by disobeying God's command not to eat from the tree of the knowledge of good and evil (Gen. 2:17).

The candles should be placed on the table in the room where the meal will be served, to spread light over the night. At least two candles (white) should be lit. One represents "creation" and the other one "redemption." They may also be symbolic of "remember" and "observe." Some say the candles glow for the harmony of the home. Others believe they encourage Sabbath joy. In some families a small pair of candles is lighted by the daughter as she begins to learn this practice from her mother. In fact, the more candles the better. This idea is taken from Genesis 1:3–4: "Then God said, 'Let there be light'; and there was light. And God saw that the light was good; and God separated the light from the darkness."

As the mother lights the candles, it is meaningful to remember that God chose another woman, Mary, to bring forth Jesus, "The light of the world" (John 8:12). Next, she rests her hands over her eyes as a covering while saying the blessing. When she opens them, her eyes are blessed by the lighted candles, fulfilling the blessing and reminiscent of the darkness and light of crea-

---

*Molly Cone, *The Jewish Sabbath* (New York: Thomas Y. Crownwell Co., 1966).

tion. The candles are to burn throughout the evening until they go out by themselves and should be enjoyed in order that the blessing not be wasted. They were blessed to shine, a reminder of the Old Testament principle, "I will bless you . . . and you will be a blessing to many others" (Gen. 12:2, TLB). What a beautiful picture rests on the table each week! Sabbath celebrates creation and redemption. The candles remind us of Jesus, the Light of the world (John 1:1, 12).

Wine: A goblet of wine is placed near the candles on the table. A sanctification prayer called the Kiddush is recited by the father (or parent) over this symbolic cup. The wine symbolizes life! The wine symbolizes joy! The cup is full! It is held at the base by the fingers, causing them to point upward. They represent the children of God, reaching up and longing for Him. It also symbolizes Christ's shed blood.

Wine had never been a part of our family's tradition before we began this celebration. The first time this cup was passed, one child made a face while swallowing it down. Another wanted two swallows. Now none of us would pass it by or skip a turn. As has been explained, if your family is unable to use wine and wishes to substitute grape juice, this can easily be done in order that the prayer may be spoken.

This prayer is an inauguration, a special ceremony of introduction, a time when Sabbath and family meet. Each member gives full attention, listening to the words of the leader. Everyone present takes a sip as the cup is passed, after the Kiddush has been spoken.

Washing: The blessing which we recite before washing our hands is intended to show gratitude to God for His sanctification of us. The prayer is a "dedication" of our hands and, through them, of ourselves to God. There is another significance. We also acknowledge that as we wash our hands and lift them up to God, our real needs are on a higher level.

One time, in my preparation for a Sabbath, I forgot to fill a bowl with water and put out a towel. But, let me be quick to add, our son, whose job it was to pass the bowl, didn't forget. This ceremony had become very important to him.

Bread: Sabbath bread is called challah (pronounced "hal-la" with a guttural "ch"), a term used in the Old Testament for new dough, which was a requirement to be presented as a "gift to the Lord" (Num. 15:17–21). May I encourage you to take the time, if at all possible, to bake your own bread for Sabbath. Traditionally, the mother prays for each member of the family as she stirs the mixture, kneading in her love. Imagine how much better it tastes when the children know that their mom was praying for them as she made the bread during the day! Children love to "punch" newly risen dough. Taking turns helping Mom shape and braid the loaf provides a good "together" time in the warm atmosphere of the kitchen. Just the fragrance that permeates the whole house is enough to make it worth your time. The unique shape, your own artistic touch, the aroma—and that's not all! Wait until you taste it! The loaves commonly braided or twisted are called "berches," which stems from the Latin word *bracellus,* meaning "arm." This suggests the type of loaf shaped like folded arms. When your arms are folded, you are at rest. You can't work. Try folding your arms tonight and really rest.

In Leviticus 24:5–9, you will discover the law that loaves of bread be placed on the altar before the Lord. According to verse 8, this was to be done on the Sabbath as a sign of the everlasting covenant between God and His people. Symbolic of that early offering, a small piece of dough, about the size of an olive, could be broken from the loaf before it is baked. Gather your children around you; toss it into the fireplace or oven and watch it burn. As you demonstrate this ancient Hebrew practice, you can use this as an opportunity to discuss Old Testament sacrifice and explain the sacrifice of Christ on the cross, finishing the work which allows us to enter into a permanent Sabbath rest.

Two loaves appear on the Sabbath table, symbolic of the double portion of manna which God provided on Fridays for the children of Israel during the years they wandered in the wilderness. Fulfilling His requirement for a rest, no manna fell on Sabbath. Read the story in Exodus 16.

The challah waits for its blessing on the table under a special covering. This cloth is symbolic of the dew that was around the camp when the Israelites woke up in the desert and were reminded again that God does provide. When the dew evaporated, behold, there on the ground lay the manna, God's provision of bread. This is even more meaningful when we remember God's provision of His Son, who said, "I am the bread of life" (John 6:48).

The covering for the bread is up to you. It could be just a paper napkin. If you want to make it special, the following are some suggestions:

A. textile paints on paper or cloth napkin
B. woodblock or potato printing on the napkin
C. a linen napkin
D. your own embroidered masterpiece—see pages 42–43

Before breaking and eating the bread, the challah are blessed. At this time knives that are on the table for the upcoming meal should be covered, symbolic of Isaiah 2:4, "And they will hammer their swords into plowshares, and their spears into pruning hooks." Christians deplore violence and long for peace. Instruments of war are to be put aside. Don't be surprised if, as you cover your knife and explain this tradition, lots of questions and a lively conversation follow. Your family should also be aware of Exodus 20:25, "And if you make an altar of stone for Me, you shall not build it of *cut* stones, for if you wield your tool on it, you will profane it." Remember, your table tonight is like an altar. On this night the bread is broken not cut, symbolizing Christ's body broken for us.

After blessing the bread, another tradition is to sprinkle a little salt on it, recalling Genesis 3:19 (NEB): "You shall gain your bread by the sweat of your brow." Finding daily bread never ceases to be a miracle, even to the farmer who works hard to produce the grain. He recognizes its ultimate source to be God's loving care for all His creatures. It is God who brings forth bread from the earth. It is customary for each person to break off his own piece, remembering that God gives us our daily bread. Jesus taught us to pray to the Father, saying, "Give us this day our daily bread" (Matt. 6:11). Each person expresses a "thank you" to God while receiving this gift. It says in Ecclesiastes 9:7 (NKJV), "Eat your bread with joy."

Grace: The grace after the meal is important. Deuteronomy 8:10 says, "When you have eaten and are satisfied, you shall bless the Lord your God for the good land which He has given you." The chapter warns that when everything is going well there is a tendency for your heart to become proud and you forget the Lord. I'm surprised at how many times we have forgotten to say "thank you," even after some super dessert! Verse 18—"But *you shall remember* the Lord your God."

Sabbath Saturday

"Joy comes in the morning" (Ps. 30:5, NKJV).

What you will need:

1. pair of white candles twisted together (page 45) and matches
2. small jar or box containing a fragrant spice (page 45)—whole cloves are great
3. small glass placed in a little bowl
4. wine or grape juice
5. Bible

How to celebrate!

Wake up Saturday morning remembering that you are in the very presence of God: "Be glad in the Lord and rejoice . . . shout for joy" (Ps. 32:11). Whatever you do today, do it "all to the glory of God" (1 Cor. 10:31). In the Hebrew tradition,

God's Word is central to this day. Read it! Study it! Meditate on the teachings of the Lord. Some families combine reading a passage from the Bible and a discussion at mealtimes (#15, page 45). In contrast to the busyness and preparations on Friday, this special Saturday should be free from pressure. Our family's purpose is not to drum up more to do, but to arrange life so that there can be a good rest from the stress and strain of the work week. All of our efforts are based on providing an enjoyable way to live out the principles found in "Remember the Sabbath day and keep it holy."

As the sun begins to go down on Sabbath afternoon, the family gathers around the table again. This meal is a simple one, something that can be prepared and served easily. It could even be just salad, dessert, and tea or coffee. After the light refreshments, the children and all grown-ups who still like to have fun go outside and watch, each wanting to see the first three stars in the evening sky, which means Sabbath is coming to a close. Help each other find them! In the twilight, Mother's (or other leader's) prayer is a farewell to the day (page 46).

The ceremony of Havdalah, which means separation, concludes the Sabbath and introduces the new week. The candles are twisted together for the service, linking symbolically the two candles of the Friday night Sabbath table which represented Creation and Redemption. They are lighted and held by one of the children. Another child holds the spice box, called the bessamen. Cloves are a nice spice to use in your little box. Pause now and read together from God's Word. Some suggestions: John 1:1–17; Luke 23:54–56; Luke 24:1–8.

Place a small glass in a little bowl. Pour wine (or grape juice) into the glass until it overflows as a visual sign of the fullness and completion of the week. As the wine spills, Sabbath departs. With head bowed, a parent (usually the father) leads the family in prayer, a benediction filled with thanksgiving to God. The twisted candle is then extinguished by dipping its flames in the spilled wine. The spice box is passed from person to person. It signifies the fragrance of life which has just been experienced in the Sabbath. The intention is that this last fragrance will carry you through the pressures of the week until you are able, once again, to celebrate Sabbath.

The symbolism in this is strikingly beautiful. When Jesus had received the sour wine on the cross and said, "It is finished" (John 19:30), He bowed His head and breathed His last. One of the soldiers pierced His side, and immediately there flowed out blood and water. During the Last Supper He said, "This cup which is poured out for you is the new covenant in My blood" (Luke 22:20). When you celebrate the weekly holy day Sabbath, when you eat the bread and drink the cup, "do this in remembrance of Me" (Luke 22:19). Praying in the garden He had said, "Father, if you are willing, take *this cup* from me; yet not my will, but yours be done" (Luke 22:42, NIV). The light of the world went out for three days, as His blood was spilled for us. Then the women prepared spices to anoint His body (Luke 23:56). Remembering that the spices signify the fragrance of life experienced in Jesus, think of His words, "I came that they might have life, and might have it abundantly" (John 10:10).

Repeat together the twenty-third Psalm: "You prepare a table before me in the presence of my enemies: You anoint my head with oil; my cup overflows" (Ps. 23:5, NIV).

There are many elements in the Sabbath celebration. Each one teaches us and reminds us of Christ:

The candles—Jesus said, "I am the light of the world" (John 8:12).

The wine—"And He took a cup and gave thanks, and gave it to them, saying, 'Drink from it, all of you; for this is My blood of the covenant'" (Matt. 26:27–28).

The dedication of hands—With His hands outstretched, lifted up on the cross, He said, "Father, into your hands I commit my spirit" (Luke 23:46, NIV).

The bread—"This is My body which is given for you; do this in remembrance of Me" (Luke 22:19).

The grace after the meal—"For of His fullness we have all received, and grace upon grace. For the law was given through Moses; grace and truth were realized through Jesus Christ" (John 1:16–17).

The twisted candles—linking Creation and Redemption. "He was in the beginning with God. All things came into being through Him" (John 1:2–3). "The true Light, that illumines every person, was coming into the world . . . to those who did receive Him, He granted ability to become God's children" (John 1:9, 12, MLB).

The overflowing cup—"This cup which is poured out for you is the new covenant in My blood" (Luke 22:20).

Putting out the candle—"It was now about the sixth hour, and darkness came over the whole land . . . the sun stopped shining. . . . Jesus called out with a loud voice, 'Father, into your hands I commit my spirit'" (Luke 23:44–46, NIV).

The spice box—"And so they took the body of Jesus, and bound it in linen wrappings with the spices, as is the burial custom of the Jews" (John 19:40).

As the Sabbath departs, its sweet scent lingers. The fragrance of His death and resurrection will carry you through the pressures of life until, "I will come again, and receive you to Myself; that where I am, there you may be also" (John 14:3).

This weekly observance represents the cycle of all history. Christ stands at the center. The Sabbath is symbolic of Christ. The Old Testament teaches "get ready to observe." Jesus, our Sabbath, enters. . . . The New Testament teaches "remember Me" with joy!

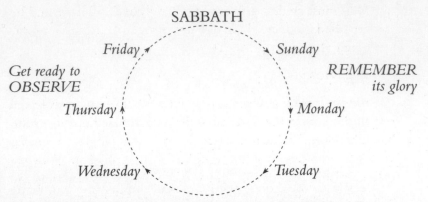

"For I, the Messiah, am Master even of the Sabbath"
(Matt. 12:8, TLB).

First Day of the Week, Sunday
The Lord's Day

What you will need:

1. big, colorful candle
2. verse cards (#18, page 46)
3. the church of your choice
4. comfortable shoes

This is why!

But on the first day of the week, at early dawn, they came to the tomb, bringing the spices which they had prepared. And they found the stone rolled away from the tomb, but when they entered, they did not find the body of the Lord Jesus. And it happened that while they were perplexed about this, behold, two men suddenly stood near them in dazzling apparel; and as the women were terrified, and bowed their faces to the ground, the men said to them, "Why do you seek the living One among the dead? He is not here, but He has risen. Remember how He spoke to you while He was still in Galilee, saying that the Son of

Man must be delivered into the hands of sinful men, and be crucified, and the third day rise again." And they remembered His words (Luke 24:1–8).

How to celebrate!

Sunday morning someone should wake up a little before the rest of the family and light a big, bright candle. Place it on the breakfast table. Beside it, prop up a card containing some special verses for the day. It is the custom of the Christian world to celebrate this first day of the week, Christ's resurrection, by going to church to worship Him and to fellowship with His people. It is helpful to be reminded that, "as was His custom, He [Jesus] entered the synagogue on the Sabbath" (Luke 4:16). Enter God's house this weekend and worship Him.

Reading on in Luke 24, on the very same day that the angels spoke to the women, the resurrected Jesus joined two men who were on the road going to the town called Emmaus. They didn't recognize Him at first. Nearing the village, the men invited Jesus to stay over. "And it came about that when He had reclined at table with them, He took the bread and blessed it, and breaking it, He began giving it to them. And their eyes were opened and they recognized Him" (vv. 30–31). *"He was recognized by them in the breaking of the bread"* (v. 35). And, "Then He opened their minds to understand the Scriptures" (v. 45). "And He led them out . . . and He lifted up His hands and blessed them" (v. 50).

Candles burn out, flowers fade away, bread gets moldy, and wine turns sour, but as He dwells in us we become His living sign to the world. He said, "You are witnesses of these things" (v. 48). Take your own Emmaus walk on Sunday afternoon, going out from your home together. "And they were conversing with each other about all these things which had taken place. And it came about that while they were conversing and discussing, Jesus Himself approached, and began traveling with them" (vv. 14–15).

In our family, Sunday night marks the end of the weekend rest. School, work, and routine activities start again on Monday morning. Sometimes we gather around the table for Havdalah service on Sunday night instead of Saturday night. Monday morning I wake up early before the rest of the family and place a lighted candle on the breakfast table. It speaks for itself as one by one family members make their way into the kitchen. Hurrying to our various responsibilities, we take with us a visual reminder that He has risen, that He is going with us through the week, and that even as the Father sent Him into the world as a witness, He has sent us to be His witnesses. You may try several plans and see what works best in your family.

Jesus said to them, "Peace be with you" (John 20:21).

Resources for Celebrating Sabbath

1. Preparation prayer

A prayer spoken by a parent (usually the mother) as the family gathers just before lighting the candles on Friday afternoon:

> Blessed are you, O Lord our God,
>> King of the Universe,
>> you are the Author of peace.
> You made the Sabbath holy,
> You called us to honor this Sabbath,
>> enter our home this night.
> Almighty God,
> Grant us and all our loved ones rest
>> on this Sabbath day.
> May the light of the candles drive out
>> from among us the spirit of anger,
>> frustration and fear.
> Send Your blessing that we may walk
>> in the ways of Your Word
>> and Your light.
> Enter our hearts this night.

Heavenly Father,
We rejoice in Your creation!
It is from you we receive every good
    and perfect gift.
Giver of life and love,
    grant us Your peace,
        through Jesus Christ our Lord. Amen.

2. Mother (or other leader) says the following blessings before lighting the candles:

Creation (lighting the first candle):

This candle represents creation.
Blessed are you, O Lord our God,
King of the Universe,
who brings forth light out of darkness.

Redemption (lighting the second candle):

This candle represents redemption.
Jesus said, "I am the light of the world."
Our Lord said, "You are the light of the world. Let your light shine before men in such a way that they may see your good works, and glorify your Father who is in heaven" (Matt. 5:14–16). As we light these candles and set them to give light to all who are in this house, light our lives with the great love of Your Son, Jesus, in whose name we pray.

3. Parent's (usually the father's) blessing (placing your hands on their heads, bless each child):

Bless your children individually according to their gifts and abilities. Include a current need (maybe an upcoming soccer game) and a future goal (the choice of a career).

4. As a compliment to his wife, the husband quotes from Proverbs 31:10, 27–30:

An excellent wife, who can find?
For her worth is far above jewels.

She looks well to the ways of her household,
And does not eat the bread of idleness.
Her children rise up and bless her;
Her husband also, and he praises her, saying:
"Many daughters have done nobly, but you excel them all."
A woman who fears the Lord, she shall be praised.

5. The family sings softly and prayerfully "Bless Our Home" (to the tune of "Edelweiss") or a similar song meaningful to your family:

Bless our home, bless our food;
Come, O Lord, and sit with us;
May our talk glow with peace,
May Your love surround us;
Friendship and love, may they bloom and grow,
Bloom and grow forever;
Bless our home, bless our food;
Come, O Lord, and sit with us.

6. The father (or leader) recites the Kiddush, the prayer of sanctification of the Sabbath, over a cup of wine or small individual glasses of grape juice:

Blessed are you, O Lord our God, King of the universe, who creates the fruit of the vine.

7. The blessing before the washing of hands:

Blessed are you, O Lord our God, King of the Universe, who has sanctified us through Your commandments and instructed us concerning the washing of hands.

8. Beginning with the leader, each person in turn repeats the Hamotzi, a blessing over the bread:

Blessed are you, O Lord our God,
    King of the Universe,
who brings forth bread from the earth.

9. Suggested menu and recipes for Friday night's Sabbath dinner:

NOTE: An asterisk in a menu means a recipe will follow.

Wine or juice • Challah*
Golden Yoich*
Baked Fish • Rice •
Carrots
Tomatoes & Greens or Candlestick Salad*
Strudel
Tea with Lemon

"A cheerful heart has a continual feast" (Prov. 15:15).

Challah
(Sabbath Bread)

2 packages dry yeast	4 tsp. salt
2 cups warm water	3 eggs, slightly beaten
¼ cup sugar	7½ cups flour
¼ cup oil	

Take a large bowl and pour in 2 cups warm water. Take your time testing to make sure it is *warm*, not hot or cool. Soften the yeast in the water. Add sugar, oil, salt. Blend in the eggs (reserve 1 tbsp. of white for brushing). Add 3 cups flour—beat well to avoid lumps. Let it rest about 5 minutes. Gradually add the rest of the flour (4½ cups). Oil the table or board you will use and your hands and knead the dough about 10 minutes.

Put the dough back into the bowl, cover with a clean cloth and leave in a warm place. Let rise about 1½ hours. Shape. Braid on cookie sheet. If you sprinkle cornmeal on the bottom of the pan, the bottom of the loaf comes out textured. Brush top with egg. Sprinkle with poppy seeds or sesame seeds. Let rise 1 hour. Bake at 375° for 30–45 minutes. Tap the bottom of each loaf. When there is a hollow sound the bread is done.

This makes two very large loaves or three average size

loaves. I braid two for the Sabbath table and make one loaf in a regular bread pan.

Variations: Take three smaller strands and braid them together. Lay them over the top of the large braided loaves. This makes a very impressive loaf of bread.

If you have sons, make several small loaves and put them at their places. Let the boys help Dad with the blessing of the bread.

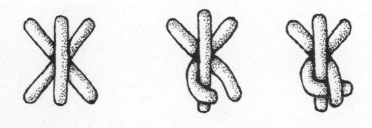

Golden Yoich
(Golden Chicken Soup)

1 large boiling chicken	1 onion, minced
10 cups water	3 stalks celery, sliced
2–3 tsp. salt	1 parsnip, sliced
3 carrots, sliced	dash of dill weed

Place chicken in a large kettle, cover with water, add salt, and bring it to a boil. Lower the temperature, and simmer the chicken until it falls off the bones. Remove, cool, bone it, and return the chicken to the broth. Add the vegetables and any others you think might taste good. Be sure to use parsnips for an especially good flavor. Cover and cook gently. This is the basic soup. You may strain the broth and serve it with noodles. We like it thick—vegetables and all.

Candlestick Salad
(Something the children can make to help with the Sabbath preparations.)

Directions for making one salad: Put a washed piece of lettuce on a plate. Place a slice of pineapple on the lettuce. Cut a banana in half in such a way that it will stand in the hole. Put half of a toothpick in the top of the banana and poke a cherry on it for the flame.

10. Grace after the meal:

Blessed are you, O Lord our God,
>   King of the Universe,
>   who provides the fruit of the earth for our use.
We bless you for fulfilling continually
>   Your promise that while the earth remains,
>   seedtime and harvest shall not fail.
Teach us to remember that it is not by bread alone that we live.
>   Grant us evermore to feed on Him who is the true
>   bread from heaven, even Jesus Christ our Lord.
O God, our Heavenly Father, look in favor
>   upon the homes of Your people.
Defend them against evil and supply all their needs
>   according to the riches of Your wonderful grace.
Make them sanctuaries of peace, love, and joy.
Help us to follow You every step of our daily lives.
May we always abide under the safe shadow of Your love,
>   through Jesus Christ our Lord. Amen.

11. Pattern for an embroidered Challah cover

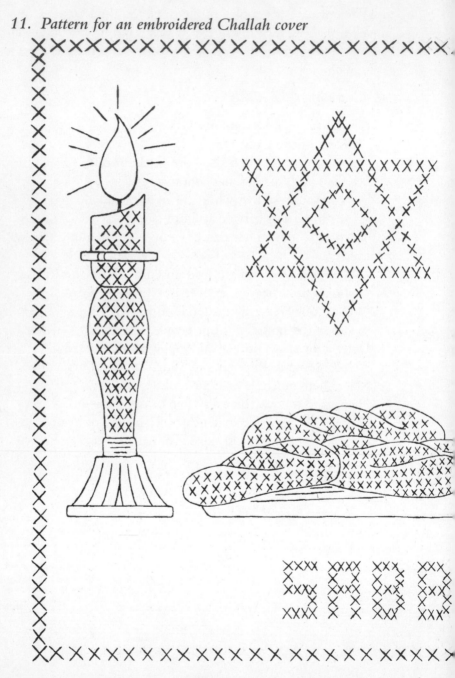

12. A centerpiece for the Sabbath table

How to make an oil float:

Select an attractive bowl. Fill half-full with water. Add a few drops of food coloring for a decorative touch. Add vegetable oil to a depth of one-half inch.

To make the floats, cut small stars out of aluminum. (We use a disposable aluminum pan.) Punch a small hole in the center of each star. Cut circles out of thin cork (available at a crafts store). Be sure to make a hole through the center of the cork. Draw the wick through the center holes in the star and cork. Float your stars in the bowl. The stars will burn until the oil is gone; then the lights will extinguish themselves. We float one star for each member of our family. All of the flames, although they are separate, share the same source, symbolic of the family depending on God for strength and life. When flowers are out of season or not available, this makes a nice centerpiece for the Sabbath table.

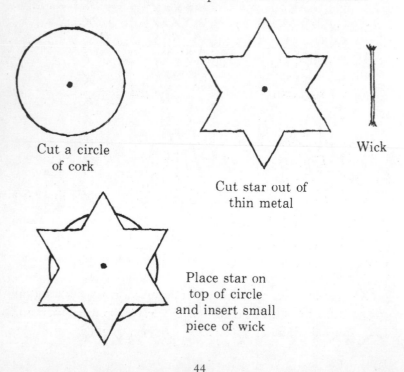

Cut a circle
of cork

Cut star out of
thin metal

Wick

Place star on
top of circle
and insert small
piece of wick

44

13. The twisted Havdalah candles:

The braided Havdalah candles used in the Sabbath celebration can be purchased in local Christian bookstores. If they do not have them in stock, they will be happy to order them for you. They are also available in Jewish bookstores.

14. Recipe for a fragrant spice; to be passed as the bessamen at the close of Sabbath:

1 cup sugar	¼ tsp. nutmeg
1 tbsp. grated orange peel	¼ tsp. cardamom
½ tsp. cinnamon	⅛ tsp. ginger

Heat oven to 200°. Mix all ingredients in 8" × 8" pan. Heat in oven, stirring occasionally, 15 minutes. Cool pan on wire rack. Pour *cooled* sugar into blender. Blend on low speed until sugar is fine. Store in tightly covered jar in cool, dry place. Use to sweeten applesauce, fresh apples, or sprinkle on pancakes, waffles, or french toast *after* you have enjoyed its fragrance at Havdalah. You might also like to try it as a sweetener in your coffee or in a cup of tea.

15. Some suggestions for family-oriented Bible study books are:

What Is a Family, by Edith Schaeffer; Baker, 1993.
Family Devotional Builder, by Karen H. Whiting; Hendrickson, 2000.
Visit your local Christian bookstore and browse the Children's section for excellent current books.

16. The food at the noonday Sabbath meal should center around cholent.

It originated on the principle that no work should be done on the Sabbath. This dish is made on Friday and simmers in a slow oven all night or in a crock pot. Try it and continue to enjoy your rest! Save dessert until late afternoon for the very lightest of the Sabbath meals.

Cholent

2–3 lbs. pot roast	5 potatoes
2 onions	5 carrots
¼ cup oil	2 tsp. salt
½ cup barley	pepper

Brown the meat in the oil. Cut up the onions and brown them lightly, too. Peel the potatoes and quarter them. Peel and slice the carrots. Combine all of the ingredients in a heavy oven-proof container with a tight-fitting lid. Cover with boiling water and place the lid securely on top. Bake this in a slow oven 250° overnight. Check from time to time and add water if necessary. It may also be cooked like a pot roast at 350° for four or five hours.

17. Mother's (or other parent's) farewell prayer:

O God of Abraham, Isaac and Jacob,
    guard your people.
The beloved Sabbath is departing.
Help us through this experience to understand
    the darkness that covered the earth
        when Your son, Jesus, died on the Cross.
Your love go with us through the night
    and wake us with Your morning light. Amen.

18. Verse cards for the Sunday morning breakfast table:

Arise, shine;
for your light has come,
And the glory of the Lord
has risen upon you (Isa. 60:1).

And when the Sabbath was over . . . very early on the first

day of the week, they came to the tomb when the sun [Son] had risen (Mark 16:1–2).

The Light shines in the darkness and the darkness did not overwhelm it (John 1:5, MLB).

19. Monday morning verses:

Now on the first day of the week
Mary announced, "I have seen the Lord" (John 20:18).

"As you sent me into the world, I have sent them into the world" (John 17:18, NIV).

"As the Father has sent Me, I also send you" (John 20:21).

Checklist for the Weekend Events

Friday

Make (or buy) bread
Clean the house
Prepare a special dinner for tonight and start the cholent
Set the table with your best
At sundown Mother (or parent) leads the family in the Preparation Prayer
Mother and oldest daughter light the Sabbath candles on the table (praying silently for the children)
Mother recites the blessing
Father (or parent) places both hands on each child and prays a blessing
Husband honors his wife with verses from Proverbs 31
The family sings a blessing
Leader blesses the cup and it is passed
Hand-washing service (a good place for the children to help)
Everyone covers up the knives with napkins
Leader removes the challah cover and blesses the bread
The bread is passed and each person breaks off a piece
Pass salt to be sprinkled on the bread

The meal is served

It's time for the grace and special prayer of thankfulness

Saturday

Read, study, discuss God's Word, perhaps at mealtime

Enjoy the day

Share a light supper

Help each other find the first three stars in the evening sky

Parent (usually the mother) closes the day with prayer

Light the two wicks on the candles that have been twisted together and let one of the children hold it

Another child holds the spice box

Read some or all of the suggested Scripture

Fill the small glass until it overflows

Read John 19:30

A parent (usually the father) leads the family in prayer

Read Luke 22:19, 20, 42

Put out the flame in the *spilled* wine or grape juice (the overflow in the dish). It is very effective at dusk, when this candle is extinguished.

Leader says, "The Light of the World went out for three days as His blood was spilled for us."

Remembering that they anointed His body with spices as was the custom, pass the spice box. Each one take a deep breath and try to remember the fragrance.

Read or say together the 23rd Psalm

Sunday

Light a big candle and place it on the breakfast table

Prop up verse cards around it

Worship the Lord in the church of your choice as a family

After the noon meal read the story of the men on the road to Emmaus, Luke 24:13–53

Take your own Emmaus walk—go out by two's or as a family

Discuss the "events of the weekend"

On the tenth of this month they are each one to take a lamb for
themselves, according to their fathers' households,
a lamb for each household.
(Exodus 12:3)

Chapter 2

Passover

In Order That You Should Remember

What Is Passover?

There are a number of ways God could have described Himself to Moses and the Hebrews at the time of the giving of the Ten Commandments (Ex. 20). He might have said: I am the Lord your God who created the heavens and the earth. Instead, "God spoke all these words, saying, 'I am the Lord your God, who brought you out of the land of Egypt, out of the house of slavery'" (Ex. 20:1–2). By God's action of redemption from physical slavery in Egypt, He called these people to be His own. "I will take you to Me for a people" and "I will be to you your God." The uniqueness of this God was His direct, personal involvement with His people. He entered their lives and showed Himself clearly. That hasn't changed. Many years later, at the same time they were celebrating the remembrance of their physical freedom, He acted again, this time providing spiritual freedom. His firstborn Son, Yeshua, became our Redeemer, sacrificed on the altar of the cross, freeing us from our slavery to sin.

As a child this concept was difficult for me to understand. In fact, I didn't understand it. I simply believed God. Crucifixions aren't written up in the daily newspaper. It all seemed so remote. And besides, how could that action take care of my guilt over sneaking a cookie? Perhaps your children feel the same way.

To understand Passover and the Cross, we need to look at the cycle of all history. With each event a grand spiral was forming, circling toward the final fulfillment of God's eternal purpose. These were not isolated events. From the beginning of time God had been saying, "There is no way to approach Me except by coming with a lamb." Sacrifice was ordained by God and instituted by Him in the beginning. Adam and Eve had never seen death. They didn't know what it was like. When they disobeyed God, He sacrificed an animal "to cover" their sin: "And the LORD God made garments of skin for Adam and his wife, and clothed them" (Gen. 3:21). Because of their eating the fruit (and even my sneaking a cookie), death had to occur. My sin must be covered in order for me to be in the presence of a holy God. He used an innocent lamb in the person of His Son to cover my guilt.

A new cycle was beginning when God tested Abraham. Calling him by name, the Lord said, "Take now your son, your only son, whom you love, Isaac, and go to the land of Moriah; and offer him there as a burnt offering on one of the mountains of which I will tell you" (Gen. 22:2). And Abraham took the wood of the burnt offering and laid it on Isaac, his son, and the two of them walked on together. Isaac questioned his father, "Where is the lamb for the offering?" And Abraham said, "God will provide for himself the lamb for the burnt offering, my son" (Gen. 22:8). What must Abraham have felt as he laid Isaac on the wood on the altar and raised his hand to slay him? Then, and only then, the Lord sent His angel to stop the sacrifice and provide a substitute, a ram caught in the thicket by his horns.

Abraham's descendants through Isaac became a great nation. In the next cycle this family of God's children had become slaves. As earth weeps, heaven answers. The Lord said to His servant Moses in the land of Egypt,

> "This month shall be the beginning of months for you; it is to be the first month of the year to you. Speak to all the congregation of Israel, saying, 'On the tenth of this month they are each one to take a lamb for themselves. . . . Your lamb shall be an unblemished male a year old. [You shall bring it into your home to dwell with you for four days.] Then the whole assembly of the congregation of Israel is to kill it at twilight. Moreover, they shall take some of the blood and put it on the two doorposts and on the lintel of the houses in which they eat it. . . . And the blood shall be a sign for you on the houses where you live; and when I see the blood I will *pass over* you. For I will go through the land of Egypt on that night, and will strike down all the first-born in the land of Egypt, both man and beast, and against all the gods of Egypt I will execute judgments—I am the LORD. Now this day will be a memorial to you, and you shall celebrate it as a feast to the LORD; throughout your generations you are to celebrate it as a *permanent* ordinance'" (Ex. 12:1–14).

In time, Moses chose priests whose main task it was to see that the people never forgot what happened the night they ate the Paschal lamb. The lamb kept alive Israel's faith in Him. The Lord told them that the firstborn of their sons should be given to Him. They should do the same with their sheep. The first-born of beasts were to be sacrificed. The first-born son was to be redeemed with a lamb (Ex. 22:29, 30; 13:11–15; 34:19–20).

One day God called to Moses, "Come up to Me on the mountain . . . and Moses entered the midst of the cloud as he went up to the mountain" (Ex. 24:12, 18). When he returned, his face shone because of his time spent with God. The law of God had been revealed. This law was personally engraved by the Almighty. God, who is holy, had set forth requirements that must be met before He could show mercy. Sin must be punished either in person or by a substitute. Lambs, goats, and rams were Israel's substitutes. The law was given to lead us to the Lamb of God. God accepts us by means of the altar.

Prophets began to appear in a new cycle. They emphasized that sacrifice is not just a ritual, a vain repetition. Jeremiah preached that it is a matter of the heart! It was meant to be an outward expression of an inner intention. It was the spirit within that gave it its value. God looks at the intentions of the heart. He was heard to say,

> "What are your multiplied sacrifices to Me? I have had enough. . . . I take no pleasure in the blood of bulls, lambs, or goats. . . . Bring your worthless offerings no longer. . . . Your hands are full of bloodshed . . . wash . . . make yourselves clean . . . cease to do evil, learn to do good. Come now, and let us reason together. Though your sins are as scarlet, they will be as white as snow; though they are red like crimson, they will be like wool" (Isa. 1:11–18).

Can you see the lamb in those words?

Gradually the prophets understood that one day God was going to send a Lamb to replace all the sacrificial lambs:

> "All of us like sheep have gone astray; each of us has turned to his own way; but the Lord has caused the iniquity of us all to fall on Him. . . . Like a lamb that is led to slaughter, and like a sheep that is silent before its shearers, so He did not open His mouth. . . . But the LORD was pleased to crush Him, putting Him to grief. . . . By His knowledge

the Righteous One, My Servant, will justify the many, as He will bear their iniquities. . . . He Himself bore the sin of many" (Isaiah 53:6–7, 10–12).

Jesus Christ, the Redeemer, is the Holy One of Israel.

Everything was ready for God to speak in the new cycle. A little baby, a Lamb, was born in a stable. He was the firstborn, an unblemished male. It was a perfect place for the Lamb to appear, and it seemed that God was making His purpose known to those who loved Him and wanted to know, those whose eyes were fixed on the Coming One. He was gently laid in a manger, where animals came to feed. There among the other lambs the little Lamb gave His first cry. An angel spoke to Joseph, "You shall call His name Jesus [Yeshua], for it is He who will save His people from their sins" (Matt. 1:21).

It was a settled conviction in the peoples' tradition that the Messiah was to be born in Bethlehem. Equally it was believed that He was to be revealed from the Migdal Eder, the "tower of the flock." This was not the watchtower for the ordinary flocks that pastured on the barren ground beyond Bethlehem, but it lay close to town, on the road to Jerusalem. The flocks that pastured there were destined for religious sacrifices. Messiah was born in the shadow of the Migdal Eder, where shepherds watched the temple flocks. Notice the deep symbolic significance.

The stable door was open to those who wanted to see Him. Shepherds came to love and adore Him, "The Lamb of God." Kings gathered to honor and worship Him, "The King of Kings." We know Him by these names.

He was taken to Jerusalem because "it is written in the law of the Lord, 'Every first-born male that opens the womb shall be called Holy to the Lord.'" While they were in the temple, a man whose name was Simeon came as he was led by the Spirit and took the child Jesus into his arms, blessed the Lord, and said, "My eyes have seen your salvation" (Luke 2:30, NIV). The Lamb continued to grow.

He was introduced into His earthly ministry with a quotation from the prophets. "Behold, the Lamb of God who takes away the *sin* of the world" (John 1:29). This was a messianic title equal to "King of Israel." The single word *sin* symbolized "totality" rather than "many" sins. John was describing the removal of the barrier that exists between God and us. It was to be the triumph of the struggle that began in Eden. Many people had gathered and were watching this event. While He was praying, the heavens rolled apart and the Holy Spirit descended upon Him in the form of a dove to anoint Him. A voice was heard, "This is My beloved Son." For these people, kings were always anointed to their office. It was the seal of God's consecration to service. Just as sheep are anointed with oil on their heads to prevent them from becoming victims of sunstroke, this double anointing was a symbol of God's protection from all opposing elements. His was to be a ministry of mercy as Savior-Lamb and a ministry of judgment as Coming King. The prophets had described this One who had come. Humiliation, trials, and agony were to precede His triumph; His countenance would be marred and His bones out of joint as He suffered and died. The prophets also projected the glories of His coming kingdom when "God with us" would take His place on the throne.

Time passed quickly, and in three and a half years the group of people that had gathered followed Him to Jerusalem: "And when He approached, He saw the city, and wept over it" (Luke 19:41). It was called "The city of the great King" (Ps. 48:2). In those days there were two ways kings entered cities. When a king came in war, his symbol was his chariot. When a king came in peace, he rode on a donkey. Ordinary people simply walked. When the Lamb rode into the city on a donkey, He was recognized by some of the people and hailed a King—the Prince of Peace. Jesus' triumphal entry into Jerusalem was the official presentation of Messiah as "King" to Israel. An echo was heard out of the past, "Rejoice greatly, O daughter of Zion!

Shout in triumph, O daughter of Jerusalem! Behold, your king is coming to you; He is just and endowed with salvation, humble, and mounted on a donkey" (Zech. 9:9).

The crowd was greatly excited by His coming—shouting and rejoicing! At last "The Coming One," the "King," had arrived to deliver them! No one noticed the shepherds leading the sheep from the Migdal Eder, the tower of the flock, from the town of Bethlehem toward the city. It was *the tenth day of Nisan,* and they were "each one to take a lamb for themselves . . . an unblemished male" (Ex. 12:3, 5). As the Lamb entered the "Home of Israel," led by a throng, the Paschal lambs were being led into the city in preparation for the Passover. Everyone knew that the way to be redeemed was to sacrifice a lamb, and the prophets had called Him "your Redeemer, the Holy One of Israel" (Isa. 48:17). But they had forgotten.

The veil of the temple trembled in readiness. The sum and substance of all good, the One in whom dwelt all the fullness of Deity in bodily form (Col. 2:9), was facing the serpent, preparing to destroy his works (Gen. 3:15; 1 John 3:8). The blood sacrifice had been a symbol of this final, once-for-all sacrifice that would redeem mankind from the curse of sin and death (Heb. 10:1–24).

Utterly defenseless, like a lamb led to the slaughter, He offered Himself, His soul and body, as a ransom, an offering, a sacrifice, for sin and sinners. The Paschal Lamb became the sacrifice of the New Covenant, which was for all (Luke 22:20).

The Lamb died, wearing a crown (John 19:2).

Pilate ordered a sign to be placed over His head: "JESUS OF NAZARETH THE KING OF THE JEWS." It appeared in the languages of all people (John 19:19, KJV).

The heavens rolled up and darkness covered the earth. A strangeness beyond understanding descended. Nothing like it had ever happened before.

On the first Lord's Day of the new cycle a Greater Light began to dawn.

I shall make "My first-born, the highest of the kings of the earth" (Ps. 89:27), for He has become "the first-born of the dead" (Rev. 1:5; Col. 1:18). For now the Lamb has been raised, "the first fruits of those who are asleep" (1 Cor. 15:20).

The rightness of the time was evident. Heaven and earth were prepared. History tells us that once this moment passed the temple was destroyed and has never been rebuilt. The priesthood ended; sacrifice could no longer be offered. The scattering of the people was total. The ancients had demanded that the Coming One present proper credentials. After the great dispersion in A.D. 70, it would have been impossible. The Lamb, standing on the altar as if slain, described as innocent, meek, and mild, represented the emblem most suited to the Messiah. There were many types of sacrifice in the Old Testament. Most were *due* and belonged to God. One was *voluntary* (John 10:17–18). This was God giving voluntarily of His own.

God sacrificed the Lamb on the altar of the cross. Those wooden beams became the doorpost for the world's home. God promises to *pass over* us with His judgment of death as we are willing to stand under its protection. This is what we remember and celebrate (see page 61) at Passover (Ex. 12:13).

Palm Sunday

What you will need:

1. stuffed lamb (toy)
2. palm branch
3. Bible

This is why!

"This month shall be the beginning of months for you; it is to be the first month of the year to you. Speak to all the congregation of Israel, saying, 'On the tenth of this month they are each one to take a lamb for themselves . . .'" (Ex. 12:2–3).

How to celebrate

We are a family of animal lovers. Currently our pet population includes two dogs and their ten puppies, four cats (four generations), and one chicken. We would thoroughly love a pet lamb too! The Lord had said to Moses that they were to take a lamb into their houses, and it was to live there with them four days. "Your lamb shall be an unblemished male a year old." Imagine! A perfect, white, soft, woolly lamb, come to live with you. We have a way of getting attached, very quickly, to our pets! "You must have it in safe keeping until the fourteenth day of this month" (Ex. 12:6, NEB), and then it was to be killed. "Go and take for yourselves lambs according to your families, and slay the Passover lamb" (Ex. 12:21b).

For your Palm Sunday celebration, choose a small stuffed lamb and place it on the table where your family gathers for meals. Prop it up on a bed of palm branches. Let this be your centerpiece for the next few days. Take time to read together Exodus 12:1–6. Talk about:

1. "Each one" needs to take a lamb, the importance of the individual act.
2. "Unblemished"—the sinless, perfect life of Christ
3. "Male"—Christ, the Son of God
4. The lamb dwelling among them—in their family, in their homes—just as Jesus dwells with us
5. It was loved before it was sacrificed, just as Jesus was loved by some before He was sacrificed.

See what other applications your family can make! Remember the words of John when he saw Jesus coming to him, "Behold, the Lamb of God who takes away the sin of the world!" (John 1:29).

The Night Before Passover

What you will need:

1. wooden spoon
2. feather
3. candle in a holder, matches
4. small paper bag
5. piece of string
6. some bread
7. Bible

How to celebrate

In the evening on the night before Passover, gather the family together. Read Exodus 12:15, 19, 42. In the Old and New Testaments leaven or fermented things often symbolize sin. Jesus warned against "the leaven of the Pharisees and Sadducees" (Matt. 16:6). Paul spoke of "the leaven of malice and wickedness" and the "unleavened bread of sincerity and truth" (1 Cor. 5:8). The Passover bread described in Exodus was to become a symbol of the sinless Christ. The instructions are clear. Unleavened bread is to be used exclusively for seven days. Orthodox Jews treat leaven during Passover like a doctor treats a contagious disease. They clean, scour, and scrub anything that might have had "contact" with leaven during the year. (We don't have to go to this extreme. We are teaching *principles,* not regulations.)

An interesting ceremony for cleaning out the leaven is performed on the evening of the day just before Passover. It is called "bedikat chametz," the search for the leaven. After dark, the father of the family (or other head of the family) leads a search through every corner of the house. It is traditional to use a wooden spoon and a feather and to be guided by the light of a candle. If the mother in the home, or whoever cleans the home, did a good job, the children would never find any leaven. It has become a tradition in our family for me to break a slice of white bread in about twelve pieces. I hide these fragments in our living room–dining room area. (Remember, the house will be dark, so they don't have to be too well hidden.) Adapt this activity to the ages of your children. Light the candle. Turn off the lights. The children join the leader, who holds the candle, to become a search team. When the light of the candle reveals one of the hidden pieces of bread, the spoon and feather are used to scoop it into the paper bag without actually touching the leaven. Remember that Christ, the light of the world, spotlights sin in our lives and offers to remove it! Because leaven represents sin, the pieces found remind us that there is not a person in the world who does only good. "All have sinned and fall short of the glory of God" (Rom. 3:23).

The first time I introduced this to our family my husband was a reluctant search team leader. I could almost see his heel marks in the carpet. After finding the fourth piece of bread he felt the spiritual impact of this activity and became an enthusiastic participant.

As you search for the leaven, think about some important concepts:

1. You can't go off alone—you need the light of Christ to find your way.
2. The light (Christ) exposes the bread (sin).
3. Mother (or whoever hides the bread) may forget where she put some of the pieces—some sins in our lives are forgotten until Christ's light shines on them.
4. Some pieces are hard to find—some of our sins are very well hidden.

Talk together, express what you are feeling, and share your impressions. You may be surprised at how much you are learning while you are having fun!

Gather the pieces into a small bag. Tie it closed with a string. Pray together in response to this experience. Include a time of silent prayer for personal confession of sin.

Turn on the lights and read Psalm 103:12.

Keep the bag overnight for use in the morning.

The Morning of Passover

What you will need:

1. the bag of bread
2. a place for a little fire
3. some matches
4. Bible

How to celebrate

On the morning of Passover, before the family leaves home for their various responsibilities, gather together with the bag of bread crumbs and some matches. We go out into our backyard or to a place where it is safe to have a small fire. A fireplace or woodstove would be suitable also.

Someone reads the Scripture:

"Do you not know that a little leaven leavens the whole lump of dough? Clean out the old leaven, that you may be a new lump, just as you are in fact unleavened. For Christ our Passover also has been sacrificed. Let us therefore celebrate the feast, not with old leaven, nor with the leaven of malice and wickedness, but with the unleavened bread of sincerity and truth" (1 Cor. 5:6–8).

Burn the bread, bag and all!

Say together: "Christ our Passover has made us unleavened. Thank you, Jesus."

I guarantee that these activities will make previously unfamiliar words in the Bible come alive with meaning.

The Lord's Passover

"In the first month, on the fourteenth day
of the month . . ."

What you will need:

1. a pair of white candles
2. Haggadah for all participants (see page 69)
3. Seder plate with all its ingredients. Small bowls on the Seder plate contain:
   a. hard-boiled egg
   b. roasted-lamb bone
   c. small bowl of salt water
   d. greens—parsley
   e. bitter herbs—horseradish
   f. charoseth, a special nut, apple, wine or grape juice mixture (recipe on page 93)
4. matzo (unleavened bread available in supermarkets), a plate for it, and three large napkins
5. wine, a common cup for family to pass and share, or a small glass of grape juice at each person's place
6. cup for Elijah
7. pillow for the father's (or other leader's) chair
8. bowl of water and towel for hand washing
9. a special dinner for the whole family (recipes on pages 93–96)

This is why!

"Now this day will be a memorial to you, and you shall celebrate it as a feast to the Lord; throughout your generations you are to celebrate it as a permanent ordinance" (Ex. 12:14).

How to celebrate

Did you know the Passover feast is for your children? "And you shall observe this event as an ordinance for you and your children forever" (Ex. 12:24).

It is for the home! The instructions say: "It is to be eaten in a single house" (Ex. 12:46).

It is repeated at least four times that God commanded Moses to instruct a father to tell the story of the Exodus to his children (Ex. 12:26–27; 13:8, 14; Deut. 6:20–21).

Exodus 12 records the events of Passover. It is included in the list we are following in Leviticus 23. The first anniversary was celebrated in Numbers 9:2–12. It was mentioned again in Numbers 28:16. It was celebrated in King Hezekiah's time (2 Chron. 30). His great-grandson, King Josiah, observed it (2 Kings 23:21–23). When Jesus was twelve years old, He went up to the temple with His parents to celebrate Passover (Luke 2:41–50). Remember when He drove the moneychangers out of the temple? That was also at Passover time (John 2:13–23).

The Passover celebration is very beautiful. The service is called "the Seder" and means "order." The intent of the ceremony is, and always has been, to obey the precept "Tell your son and daughter." It is a *very* impressive way to teach your children, as you will discover! Many churches introduce Passover as a "church family" celebration. Once you have participated in a church Seder service you will want to lead *your* family through this experience. All ages should be represented, if possible. Each generation has a place and purpose to fulfill. The children must understand, and this requires the wisdom of adults. Central to the celebration is the symbolic meal to which the entire extended family is invited and around which they come together. Great care and attention should be given to encourage your children's participation. Meaningful explanations must be given to them. Take time for this.

Each person should bring a jacket or sweater to his place at the table in keeping with Exodus 12:11: "Your sandals on your feet, and your staff in your hand." It will be a reminder to us that we should be "ready" to follow and obey the Lord wherever and whenever He calls. "Be dressed in readiness, and keep your lamps alight" (Luke 12:35).

The table is covered with a white cloth. Using your best dishes, set places for each member of the family. One extra setting and chair is reserved for Elijah the prophet, who came as John the Baptist (Matt. 11:14; Luke 1:17). Traditionally it is the mother who lights the candles at all of the festival celebrations (see chapter 1).

In the early days only free men were privileged to recline around a table to eat their meals. Place a pillow at the back of the chair where the leader of the Seder will sit to signify our physical and spiritual freedom.

A copy of the Haggadah (see page 69) for every one or two readers makes the ceremony move more smoothly.

Passover Symbols and Their Meanings

Haggadah:

Haggadah means narration or recital. It is the name given to the text used for narrating the story of the Exodus, which is the core of the Seder ceremony. Stories are such a wonderful way of communicating a message. The central activity of Passover is the retelling of a story. The whole point is to "remember the deeds of the Lord" and "teach it to your children." Modern educators agree that audio-visual techniques (which are *centuries* old) have real merit. For a good discussion, ask, "What do you remember about leaving Egypt?" Retell the story in your own words. Then ask the same question, substituting the words *bondage* or *slavery* for "Egypt." Discuss freedom and what it means in our time. The Liberty Bell is inscribed with Leviticus 25:10 (KJV), "And ye shall . . . proclaim liberty throughout all the land."

Kiddush:

Holding the first cup of wine or juice in his right hand, the leader begins the Seder by reciting the Kiddush, which means consecration. Wine is a symbol of joy (Ps. 104:15) and is therefore to remind us of the joy that is ours as a result of our salvation.

The Invitation:

The Haggadah begins with words of hope and promise. "Our fathers knew affliction in Egypt, yet they were redeemed." This passage emphasizes that redemption is available no matter how difficult your present situation. An invitation follows: "Let all who are hungry come in and eat; let all who are in need join us as we celebrate this Passover feast."

Jesus says, "Come to Me, all who are weary and heavy-laden, and I will give you rest" (Matt. 11:28).

Washing of Hands:

A pitcher of water, a basin, and a towel are brought to the table. The head of the house washes and dries his hands. This imitates the priest who washed before entering into the Holy of Holies. Jesus used this occasion to teach His disciples a lesson in humility by washing their feet (John 13). We also acknowledge that as we wash our hands and lift them up to God, our real needs are on a higher level.

Karpas:

Taking a piece of parsley, the leader dips it in the salt water and gives it to each member of the family, keeping a piece for himself. The meaning of this act is to show how God brought them safely across the Red Sea (salt water) and made them a new nation (green vegetable).

Matzo:

The three loaves of unleavened bread represent the Trinity. Each loaf is wrapped in a napkin. The middle loaf is a perfect picture of Christ in the Passover. The father breaks the middle loaf into two parts. He puts half of it back between the two loaves and carefully wraps the other half in the napkin and places it under the pillow. The unleavened bread is broken, symbolic of the death of Jesus. When the broken piece is wrapped in a linen napkin and placed under the pillow, His burial in a borrowed tomb is dramatized. The resurrection is symbolized at the close of the Seder when this hidden loaf is brought back to the table.

Unleavened bread is made of pure flour and water without yeast to ferment and sour it. Yeast vividly pictures what sin does to a life. There can be no minimum quantity tolerated in our lives, just as there is no minimum quantity of leaven that can be allowed to remain in the loaf. The slightest crumb is forbidden because it will eventually spoil the bread in which it is mixed. After the dough is flattened, it is pierced through with a pointed instrument to keep it from bubbling under the flame. John 19:37 speaks of Christ, whose body was pierced by the nails. This piercing of the Messiah is foretold by the Old Testament prophets. In Psalm 22:16 it says, "They pierced my hands and my feet." In Zechariah 12:10 it is said of the Jewish people that at Christ's second coming, "They will look on Me whom they have pierced."

The Passover Lamb:

The children of Israel were told how to protect themselves from the last plague. Each family was to take a lamb and kill it and drain the blood into a basin; then they were to take a bunch of hyssop, dip it into the blood, and strike the upper lintel and two side doorposts of the house where they would be eating the lamb (Ex. 12:21–22). "And the blood shall be a sign for you on the houses where you live; and when I see the blood I will pass over you, and no plague will befall you to destroy you, when I strike the land of Egypt" (Ex. 12:13). Thus, making the sign of the cross on each door, a refuge against physical and spiritual death was provided.

But why did the children of Israel need to be protected against the angel of death who was sent out to execute judgment upon the oppressor? The answer can be found throughout Scripture: "There is not a just righteous man on earth who does what is right and never sins" (Eccles. 7:20, NIV). "The soul who sins is the one who will die" (Ezek. 18:20, NIV). Every human being who fails to live up to the moral law of God is guilty and has to pay with his life. The blood of an innocent lamb became the symbol of an innocent life covering a guilty life from the eyes of a holy and just God. "When I see the blood, I will pass over you." The prophecy of Isaiah 53:7 says that He (the Messiah) is brought as "a lamb that is led to slaughter." John, seeing Jesus, said, "Behold, the Lamb of God who takes away the sin of the world!" (John 1:29).

Prophecy and history meet. "For Christ our Passover also has been sacrificed" (1 Cor. 5:7).

The Shank Bone and the Egg:

Hebrew people, since the destruction of the temple, are unable to observe the Passover according to the law of Moses. That law said the Passover lamb was to be offered *only* in the tabernacle where God placed His name (Deut. 16:5–6; 1 Kings 9:3). God allowed the destruction of the place where the Passover lamb could be offered, because the Messiah who was to take the place of the Passover lamb has already come. In the years that followed, the Jews have provided a symbol for the Passover lamb by placing a roasted lamb shank bone on a plate. To it the rabbis added an egg. This is to be a reminder of the Hagigah, which was the "voluntary peace offering" on the second day of Passover. All of this directs us to Christ. Through His death, symbolized by the shank bone, He voluntarily offered Himself, making peace with God, reconciling us to Him. "God was in Christ reconciling the world to Himself" (2 Cor. 5:19).

The Questions:

I believe the questions in the Haggadah are meant to be suggestions, not an exhaustive list. Encourage everyone to ask questions. In response to the questions, two points are made clear: each individual has to consider himself redeemed, and the redemption was accomplished by God, personally.

Charoseth:

This is a mixture of coarsely chopped fruit and spices which resembles, in color, the clay or mortar that the Israelites made in Egypt.

Maror:

Bitter herbs are symbolic of slavery and misery. To us as Christians, the eating of bitter herbs also reminds us of the bitter cup our Lord tasted on our behalf.

Shulhan Orekh:

The meal is eaten and enjoyed. It begins with a hard-boiled egg in salt water. The egg represents the hardness of Pharaoh's heart. The salt water symbolizes the tears of the Hebrew slaves under Egypt's bondage.

Afikoman:

This is the broken piece of matzo that was hidden away early in the service. Meaning "dessert," it is to be eaten at the end of the meal. No food should follow it, so that the taste will linger.

When this loaf was broken at the start of the service, it symbolized the breaking of the body of the Son of God who is our High Priest (Psalm 110). When the loaf was wrapped in linen, it spoke prophetically of the wrapping of the body of Christ in linen after the Crucifixion. When the broken and wrapped bread was put under the pillow, it symbolized His burial in the sepulcher of Joseph of Arimathea (Matt. 27:57–60). Now after the meal is over, the pillow is removed, reminding us of the stone that was removed by the angel (Matt. 28:1–2). Then the wrapped loaf is taken out and unwrapped. It signifies the Resurrection. The bread is broken into small pieces and every member of the family takes one and eats it. This signifies the believer feeding upon the Bread of Life, the Lord Jesus Christ (John 6:35). And when He had taken some bread and given thanks, He broke it, and gave it to them, saying, "This is My body which is given for you" (Luke 22:19).

Alert the children to watch where this is hidden so that they can help find it. Each person must find Christ for himself (Ex. 12:3).

Grace:

Grace comes after the meal. "When you have eaten and are satisfied, you shall bless the Lord your God" for all that He has given you (Deut. 8:10).

The Cup of Elijah:

After drinking the fourth cup of wine or juice, pour Elijah's cup and have the children open the door.

If you would ask why, you would be told that Elijah, in the person of John the Baptist, will come in to announce that the Messiah has come. All through the service the hope of His coming is expressed. The open door is to admit Elijah, the forerunner of the Messiah (Mal. 3:1; 4:5). At one end of the table stands a cup. It is in front of a chair that no one occupies. It is said that this is for Elijah.

Passover is a time for "telling," "traditions," "ritual," and "celebration." The purpose of the Seder is to provide families with the opportunity to consider the dramatic and miraculous events that led to the Exodus over 3,000 years ago. The God of Abraham changed the lives of His people when He rescued them from slavery under the Egyptian Pharaohs. He became God their Savior. It is no wonder they remembered and celebrated the event every year.

Then at one of those routine Passovers many years later, while the priests were slaughtering lambs in the temple, Pontius

Pilate turned over Yeshua to be sacrificed on the cross and God's salvation was complete. Think about it tonight.

Resources for Celebrating Passover
The Haggadah for Christians—A Guide for Celebrating the Biblical Feast of Passover

For your convenience, a printable copy of this guide can be found on our Web site (*www.bethanyhouse.com*). Just type in the name of this book in the "Search" box.

Introduction

Before the service begins, the wine or grape juice is poured and the symbolic foods are placed on the table in front of the leader. The references for the Scriptures do not need to be read aloud.

Leader (traditionally the father of the family):

Welcome to our Passover Seder. Tonight we have gathered to tell the story that has been repeated every year for more than 3,000 years. We are remembering an event when God acted on behalf of his people, rescuing them from bondage in Egypt.

As Christians, we are also remembering another event when God acted, rescuing all people from spiritual bondage. It took place during the annual celebration of Passover and is a continuation of the story of God's love.

Let us begin by hearing the words of instruction from Scripture:

Participant:

The Lord said to Moses, "These are the Lord's appointed feasts, the sacred assemblies you are to proclaim at their appointed times: The Lord's Passover begins at twilight on the fourteenth day of the first month" (Lev. 23:1, 4–5, NIV).

Participant:

"This is a day you are to commemorate; for the generations to come you shall celebrate it as a festival to the

Lord—a lasting ordinance. It is the Passover sacrifice to the Lord, who passed over the houses of the Israelites in Egypt and spared our homes when he struck down the Egyptians" (Ex. 12:14, 27, NIV).

Family/Group:

On the first day of the Feast of Unleavened Bread, the disciples came to Jesus and asked, "Where do you want us to make preparations for you to eat the Passover?" He replied, "Go into the city to a certain man and tell him, 'The Teacher says: My appointed time is near. I am going to celebrate the Passover with my disciples at your house.'" So the disciples did as Jesus had directed them and prepared the Passover. (Matt. 26:17–19, NIV)

Lighting the Celebration Candles

Leader:

Our Seder begins with the lighting of candles and with prayers of praise and blessing.

Woman (traditionally the mother of the family):

The candles are lit as the blessing is recited.

Lighting the first candle: We praise you, O Lord our God, King of the Universe, who brings forth light out of darkness.

Lighting the second candle: Jesus said, "I am the light of the world."

As I light these candles and place them to give light to all who are in this room, light our lives with the great love of your Son, Jesus.

Leader:

Four times during the Seder service, we drink from a cup of wine or grape juice. The first cup is called the Cup of Sanctification.

Kiddush

Leader (holding the cup):

We praise you, O Lord our God, creator of the fruit of the vine.

We praise you, O Lord our God, King of the Universe, who has chosen us out of all the people of the world and made us holy through your Word. With love you have given us commandments to follow, which include festivals for rejoicing, holidays for gladness, and Sabbaths for rest. In this feast of Passover you provide an annual remembrance of our freedom and deliverance from Egypt. You have chosen us. You have given us this holy festival with loving-kindness and have blessed us with your favor.

We praise you, O Lord our God, King of the Universe, for giving us life and sustaining us so that we may celebrate this season of joy.

The cup is a symbol of joy. Let us drink from it and be reminded of the joy that is ours as a result of our salvation.

All drink from the first cup, the Cup of Sanctification.

Washing of Hands

Leader:

Traditionally, the high priest washed his hands before entering the Holy of Holies. For us this is a reminder of our need to be cleansed by Christ.

A bowl of water and a towel are offered to all participants to wash their hands.

Karpas

Leader:

Parsley and salt water remind us that God brought His people safely through the Red Sea (salt water) and made them a new nation (green vegetable).

The leader dips some parsley into salt water. Each person takes a piece.

The following blessing is spoken before eating the Karpas.

Leader:

We praise you, O Lord our God, King of the Universe, who creates the produce of the earth. Thank you for all of the ways you have cared for your people through the centuries.

All eat the Karpas (parsley).

The Bread

Leader:

There are three loaves of unleavened bread on the table. They are called a Unity. As Christians we realize that this is the unique unity of God: Father, Son, and Holy Spirit.

The middle piece of unleavened bread represents Christ, the second person of the Trinity. As I break this piece in two, be reminded of His broken body and His death. I will wrap the larger piece in a napkin and hide it under a pillow. It is called the Afikomen (aph-e-qo-man). Christ's burial is dramatized in this act. Then I will put the other piece back into the fold of the napkin.

The leader carries out these instructions.

The Invitation

Family/Group:

This is the bread of affliction, which our ancestors ate in the land of Egypt. Let all who are hungry come in and eat; let all who are in need join us as we celebrate this Passover feast.

Leader:

The second cup is called the Cup of Instruction.

The Questions

It is traditional for the youngest child present to ask the following questions. In some celebrations several children take turns so that more may participate.

Child:

Why is this night different from all other nights? On other nights we eat either leavened or unleavened bread; why on this night only unleavened bread?

On all other nights we eat any kind of green vegetables; why on this night must it be a bitter one?

On all other nights we don't dip the vegetables in salt water; why on this night do we dip them?

On all other nights we eat in an ordinary manner; why on this night do we dine with a special ceremony and put a pillow at our leader's place?

Leader:

"And you shall observe this event as an ordinance for you and your children forever" (Exodus 12:24).

Child:

"And when your children ask you, 'What does this ceremony mean to you?'" (Exodus 12:26, NIV).

Leader:

"Then tell them, 'It is the Passover sacrifice to the Lord, who passed over the houses of the Israelites in Egypt and spared our homes when he struck down the Egyptians'" (Exodus 12:27, NIV).

The Reply

Family/Group:

We were Pharaoh's slaves in Egypt, and the Lord our God rescued us with a mighty hand and an outstretched arm. And if the Lord had not brought our forefathers out of Egypt, then we, our children, and our children's children would be slaves.

Leader:

Our children have asked, "Why do we put a pillow at our leader's place?"

The chair in which our leader reclines is luxurious with a pillow symbolizing the spirit of freedom and comfort that is found in our homes tonight because we are no longer slaves serving taskmasters but free men and women seated around this table.

Family/Group:

We who are Christians can rejoice as we keep the Passover in remembrance of our own slavery to sin. We know that with a mighty hand and an outstretched arm the Lord our God rescued us.

So that is why, even though we might all be wise, learned, full of experience and understanding, knowing God's Word well, it is still our responsibility to tell the story of the going out from Egypt and to praise the Lord.

Leader:

The Lord said to Moses and Aaron in Egypt, "This month is to be for you the first month . . . of your year. Tell the whole community of Israel that on the tenth day of this month each man is to take a lamb for his family, one for each household. If any household is too small for a whole lamb, they must share one with their nearest neighbor, having taken into account the number of people there are. You are to determine the amount of lamb needed in accordance with what each person will eat. The animals you choose must be year-old males without defect, and you may take them from the sheep or the goats.

Take care of them until the fourteenth day of the

month, when all the people of the community of Israel must slaughter them at twilight. Then they are to take some of the blood and put it on the sides and tops of the doorframes of the houses where they eat the lambs.

That same night they are to eat the meat roasted over the fire, along with bitter herbs, and bread made without yeast.

This is how you are to eat it: with your cloak tucked into your belt, your sandals on your feet and your staff in your hand. Eat it in haste; it is the Lord's Passover" (Ex. 12:3–11, NIV).

The Israelites did just what the Lord commanded Moses and Aaron.

At midnight the Lord struck down all the firstborn in Egypt, from the firstborn of Pharaoh, who sat on the throne, to the firstborn of the prisoner, who was in the dungeon, and the firstborn of all the livestock as well. Pharaoh and all his officials and all the Egyptians got up during the night, and there was loud wailing in Egypt, for there was not a house without someone dead. (Exodus 12:29–30, NIV)

Introduction

(to the Midrash, which is the heart of the story)

Family/Group:

We praise you, O God, for keeping your promise to Israel. For the Lord planned in advance the end of the bondage, doing what He promised Abraham in the covenant: "Know for certain that your descendants will be strangers in a country not their own, and they will be enslaved and mistreated four hundred years. But I will punish the nation they serve as slaves, and afterward they will come out with great possessions" (Genesis 15:13–14, NIV).

The Midrash

Leader:

My father and his family went down to Egypt and sojourned there. We were few in number when we went, only seventy people. We moved there because there was a famine in Canaan and we needed food and pasture for our flocks. Joseph arranged with Pharaoh for us to sojourn in the land of Goshen.

While we were there, we became a nation. We multiplied and became like the stars of heaven. We grew strong, great, and powerful, and the Egyptians were afraid. They mistreated us and made us suffer. We cried to the Lord, the God of our fathers, and the Lord heard our voice, saw our affliction, toil, and oppression, and God remembered His covenant with Abraham, Isaac, and Jacob. The Lord brought us forth out of Egypt with a mighty hand and an outstretched arm and awesome power, and with signs and wonders (from Genesis 47:4; Deuteronomy 10 and 26; Exodus 1 and 2).

Family/Group:

The Lord brought us out of Egypt.

Leader:

"On that same night I will pass through Egypt and strike down every firstborn—both men and animals—and I will bring judgment on all the gods of Egypt. I am the Lord" (Exodus 12:12, NIV).

Family/Group:

With "a mighty hand" means the cattle blight (disease).

Leader:

"The hand of the Lord will bring a terrible plague on your livestock in the field—on your horses and donkeys and camels and on your cattle and sheep and goats" (Exodus 9:3, NIV).

Family/Group:

With "an outstretched arm" means redemption.

Leader:

"I will redeem you with an outstretched arm and with mighty acts of judgment" (Exodus 6:6, NIV).

Family/Group:

And "with great awe" means His divine presence.

Leader:

"Where else will you ever find another example of God's removing a nation from its slavery by sending terrible plagues, mighty miracles, war and terror? Yet that is what the Lord your God did for you in Egypt, right before your very eyes" (Deuteronomy 4:34, TLB).

Family/Group:

And "with signs" means the staff of Moses.

Leader:

"Take this staff in your hand so you can perform miraculous signs with it" (Exodus 4:17, NIV)

Family/Group:

And "with wonders" means the blood,

Leader:

"Take some of the blood and put it on the sides and tops of the doorframes of the houses where they eat the lambs" (Exodus 12:7, NIV).

Leader and Family/Group:

The ten plagues that the Lord brought upon the Egyptians are these: blood, frogs, lice, flies, cattle blight, boils, hail, locusts, darkness, and slaying of the firstborn.

It is our prayer tonight that God will cast out the plagues that surround and threaten us, beginning in our own hearts.

We Should Have Been Content

Leader and Family/Group alternate (bold for Family/Group):

Leader:

God has blessed us so many times with acts of kindness.

If He had rescued us from Egypt, but not punished the Egyptians,

we should have been content.

If He had punished the Egyptians, but not destroyed their gods,

we should have been content.

If He had destroyed their gods, but not have killed their firstborn,

we should have been content.

If He had killed their firstborn, but not given us their property,

we should have been content.

If He had given us their property, but not divided the Red Sea before us,

we should have been content.

If He had divided the Red Sea before us, but not brought us through it dry,

we should have been content.

If He had brought us through the sea dry, but not supplied us in the desert for forty years,

we should have been content.

If He had supplied us in the desert for forty years, but not fed us with manna,

we should have been content.

If He had fed us with manna, but not given us the Sabbath,

we should have been content.

If He had given us the Sabbath, but not brought us to Mount Sinai,

we should have been content.

If He had brought us to Mount Sinai, but not given us the Torah,

we should have been content.

If He had given us the Torah, but not brought us to the Land of Promise,

we should have been content.

If He had brought us to the Land of Promise, but not built us the Temple,

we should have been content.

If He had built us the Temple, but not provided permanent salvation,

we should have been content.

But, praise the Lord! God provided permanent salvation through the sacrifice of our Messiah.

Leader and Family/Group:

Then how much more, doubled and redoubled, is the claim the Lord has upon our thankfulness! For He took us out of Egypt, and punished the Egyptians, and destroyed their gods, and killed their firstborn, and gave us their property, and tore the Sea apart for us, and brought us through it dry, and supplied our needs in the desert for forty years, and fed us with manna, and gave us the Sabbath, and brought us to Mount Sinai, and gave us the Torah, and brought us to the Land of Promise, and built the temple of his choosing, and provided permanent salvation through the sacrifice of our Messiah, making atonement for all our sins.

Passover Sacrifice, Unleavened Bread, and Bitter Herbs

Leader:

There are three symbols in the Passover Seder that are so important that no Seder is complete unless they are explained.

Rabbi Gamaliel used to say: "Whoever does not make mention of these essentials of the Passover Seder has not fulfilled his duty: the Passover Sacrifice, unleavened bread, and bitter herbs."

Leader (holding up the shank bone):

The Passover Sacrifice, the lamb which our ancestors ate during the time when the temple still stood—what was the reason for it?

Family/Group:

"It is the Passover sacrifice to the Lord, who passed over the houses of the Israelites in Egypt and spared our homes when he struck down the Egyptians" (Exodus 12:27, NIV).

Leader:

The children of Israel were told how to protect themselves from the last plague. Each family was to take a lamb and kill it and drain the blood into a basin; and then take a bunch of hyssop and dip it in the blood and strike the upper lintel and the two side doorposts of the house. "The blood will be a sign for you on the houses where you are; and when I see the blood, I will pass over you. No destructive plague will touch you when I strike Egypt" (Exodus 12:13, NIV). By making the sign of the cross on each door, a refuge against death was provided.

But why did the children of Israel need to be protected against the angel of death who was sent out to execute judgment upon the oppressor?

Family/Group:

The answer can be found throughout Scripture: "There is not a righteous [person] on earth who does what is right and never sins" (Ecclesiastes 7:20, NIV).

"The soul who sins is the one who will die" (Ezekiel 18:20, NIV).

Every person who fails to live up to the moral law of God

is guilty and has to pay with his or her life. The blood of an innocent lamb became the symbol of an innocent life covering a guilty life from the eyes of a holy and just God. The prophecy of Isaiah 53:7 reads, "He [Messiah] was led like a lamb to the slaughter." John the Baptist, seeing Jesus, said, "Look, the Lamb of God, who takes away the sin of the world!" (John 1:29, NIV).

Leader:

Prophecy and history meet.

Family/Group:

"For Christ, our Passover lamb, has been sacrificed" (1 Corinthians 5:7, NIV).

Leader (holding up the unleavened bread):

This is the unleavened bread that we will eat. Our children have asked, "What is the reason for it?"

Family/Group:

It is because there was not enough time for our ancestors' dough to rise when the Lord redeemed them. As it says, "With the dough they had brought from Egypt, they baked cakes of unleavened bread. The dough was without yeast because they had been driven out of Egypt and did not have time to prepare food for themselves" (Exodus 12:39, NIV).

Leader:

The unleavened bread is a picture of Christ. It is made of pure flour and water—without yeast to ferment and sour it. Yeast is a vivid symbol of sin and what it does to a human life. After the dough is flattened, before it is baked, it is pierced and striped with a pointed tool to keep it from bubbling under the flame. The Gospels report they crucified Jesus. Psalm 22:16–18 (NIV) says, "They have pierced my hands and my feet. I can count all my bones; people stare and gloat over me. They divide my garments among them and cast lots for my clothing." John 19:33–34 (NIV) reports, "They did not break his legs. Instead, one of the soldiers pierced Jesus' side with a spear. . . ." The prophecy of Zechariah 12:10 (NIV) was fulfilled: "They will look on me, the one they have pierced, and they will mourn for him as one mourns for an only child, and grieve bitterly for him as one grieves for a firstborn son." The prophecy of Isaiah 53:5 (NIV) declares, "He was pierced for our transgressions, he was crushed for our iniquities; the punishment that brought us peace was upon him, and by his wounds we are healed."

Leader lifts the bitter herbs:

These are the bitter herbs that we will eat. Our children have asked, "What is the reason for them?"

Family/Group:

It is because the Egyptians made the lives of our ancestors in Egypt so bitter and miserable. As it is said, "They made their lives bitter with hard labor in brick and mortar and with all kinds of work in the fields; in all their hard labor the Egyptians used them ruthlessly" (Exodus 1:14, NIV).

Leader:

These bitter herbs, called *maror* (ma-ror), are symbolic of the bitterness of slavery and the miserable existence in Egypt. To us as Christians, the eating of bitter herbs reminds us of our lives before we knew the Savior. The *maror* also symbolizes the bitter cup our Lord tasted on our behalf. The horseradish brings tears to our eyes as we taste it and remember.

Family/Group:

On that day tell your son [children], "I do this because of what the Lord did for me when I came out of Egypt" (Exodus 13:8, NIV).

Leader:

Our children have asked, "Why do we dip green vegetables in salt water?"

Family/Group:

The meaning of this act is to show how God brought the children of Israel safely through the Red Sea (salt water) and made of them a new nation (green vegetables).

In every generation let all look on themselves as if each one, individually, came forth out of Egypt. It was not only our ancestors that the Lord redeemed, but He redeemed us as well.

As it says, "He brought us out from there to bring us in and give us the land that he promised on oath to our forefathers" (Deuteronomy 6:23, NIV).

We are therefore duty-bound to praise, thank, glorify, and exalt, honor, bless, and adore Him who performed all these miracles for our ancestors and for us. He brought us out of slavery into freedom, out of misery into joy, out of mourning into rejoicing, out of darkness into His light, and out of bondage into redemption. Let us praise Him!

"For God so loved the world that he gave his one and only Son, that whoever believes in him shall not perish but have eternal life" (John 3:16, NIV).

The Hallel

Leader and Family/Group alternate (group in bold):

Leader:

Praise the Lord! Praise, O servants of the Lord.
Praise the name of the Lord.
Blessed be the name of the Lord
from this time forth and forever.
From the rising of the sun to its setting
the name of the Lord is to be praised.
The Lord is high above all nations,

His glory is above the heavens.

Who is like the Lord our God, who is enthroned on high,

who humbles Himself to behold the things that are in heaven and in the earth?

He raises the poor from the dust, and lifts the needy from the ash heap,

to make them sit with princes, with the princes of His people.

Praise the Lord!

Let us all drink from the second cup, the Cup of Instruction.

The Symbolic Meal

A bowl of water and a towel are offered to all participants to wash their hands.

Leader:

Before we eat, let us wash our hands and say together:

Family/Group:

We praise you, O Lord our God, King of the Universe, for this reminder of our need to be cleansed by you.

Leader breaks pieces from the upper and middle loaves of unleavened bread and passes them. Each participant takes a piece. The following blessing is spoken.

Leader:

We praise you, O Lord our God, King of the Universe, who brings forth bread from the earth.

We praise you, O Lord our God, King of the Universe, who sanctified us and commanded us concerning the eating of unleavened bread.

Let us all eat this unleavened bread.

The leader breaks the bottom piece of unleavened bread. It is passed and each participant takes two pieces and makes a "Hillel Sandwich" with some horseradish, the bitter herb, and charoseth.

Leader:

We praise you, O Lord our God, King of the Universe, who sanctified us and commanded us concerning the eating of bitter herbs.

Family/Group:

"They are to eat it [the Lamb] with unleavened bread and bitter herbs" (Numbers 9:11).

Leader:

Let us eat this symbolic sandwich and remember.

Dinner

Leader:

It is customary to begin our meal with a hard-cooked egg splashed with salt water. The egg represents the hardness of Pharaoh's heart. The salt water symbolizes the tears of the Hebrew slaves under the bondage of the Egyptian taskmasters.

Dinner is served.

After dinner the Seder continues.

Leader:

According to the directions from the Hebrew Passover Haggadah (Hag-ga-da), the eating of the *Afikoman* (aph-e-qo-man)—the hidden loaf—is next. The Haggadah says, "The eating of the *Afikoman* is an essential part of our Seder service, for it is a reminder of the Paschal lamb." The prayer says it is eaten "in memory of the Passover sacrifice." Who can find the *Afikoman?*

Let one of the children find it behind the pillow and give it to the leader.

Leader:

This is the broken piece of unleavened bread that was hidden away early in the service. *Afikoman* means "dessert." It is to be eaten at the end of the meal. No food should follow it, so the taste will linger.

When this loaf was broken at the start of the service, it symbolized the breaking of the body of the Son of God, who is our High Priest. When the loaf was wrapped in linen, it spoke prophetically of the wrapping of the body of Christ in linen after the Crucifixion. When the broken and wrapped bread was put under the pillow, it symbolized His burial in the sepulcher of Joseph of Arimathea (Matt. 27:57–60). Now after the meal is over, the pillow is removed, symbolizing the stone that was removed by the angel (Matt. 28:1–2). Then the wrapped loaf was taken out and unwrapped, symbolizing the Resurrection. The bread is broken into small pieces, and every participant takes a piece. This symbolizes the believer feeding upon the Bread of Life, the Lord Jesus Christ (John 6:35). Jesus made this *Afikoman* the symbol of His broken body as a sacrifice for our sins. Each person must find Christ individually.

The leader breaks the Afikoman into small pieces. They are passed to each participant.

Leader:

This is the place in the Passover service that is recorded for us in the New Testament. Jesus, our Messiah, "took bread, gave thanks and broke it, and gave it to them saying, 'This is my body given for you; do this in remembrance of me'" (Luke 22:19, NIV).

All eat a piece of unleavened bread.

Leader:

When you have eaten and are satisfied, praise the Lord your God for all that He has given you (from Deuteronomy 8:10).

Grace

Leader:

The third cup is called the Cup of Redemption.
Let us say the blessing.

Family/Group:

May the name of the Lord be praised from now to eternity.

Leader:

Let us praise Him whose food we have eaten.

Family/Group:

We praise you, O Lord our God, for the food we have eaten. It is from you we receive every good and perfect gift, and through your goodness we live. We praise you, O Lord our God, King of the Universe, who feeds the entire world with your goodness, with grace, loving-kindness, and compassion. You give bread to all. You give Christ to all, for your mercy is forever.

Let us give thanks to you, O Lord our God, for food with which you feed and sustain us continually, at all times and at every hour.

Take pity, O Lord our God, on Israel, your people, and on Jerusalem, your city, and on Zion, the dwelling place of your glory, and on the kingdom of the House of David, your anointed.

Our God and Father, shepherd us, feed us, maintain us, sustain us, and ease us from all our troubles.

Let us not be needing gifts at the hands of flesh and blood, but only at your hand, that is full and open, holy and broad.

Leader (lifting the third cup):

This cup is called the Cup of Redemption. It is to be shared after the meal. The Lord said, "I will redeem you with an outstretched arm." This is the place in the Passover service that is recorded for us in the New Testament, where it says, "In the same way, after supper, Jesus took the cup, saying, 'This cup which is poured out for you is the new covenant in my blood. Take this and share it among yourselves'" (from Luke 22:20, 17).

Let us all drink the third cup, the Cup of Redemption.

The Hallel

Leader:

The fourth cup is called the Cup of Praise.

Leader and Family/Group alternate

(Family/Group in bold):

> Not unto us, O Lord, not unto us;
> **but unto your name be the glory.**
> For your great mercy and kindness
> **and for your truth's sake.**
> Why do the nations say,
> **"Where is their God?"**
> Our God is in heaven;
> **He does whatever pleases Him.**
> Their idols are silver and gold,
> **made by human hands.**
> They have mouths, but cannot speak;
> **they have eyes, but cannot see.**
> They have ears but cannot hear;
> **they have a nose, but cannot smell.**
> Their hands cannot feel;
> **their feet cannot walk;**
> they can make no sound with their throat.
> **I love the Lord because He hears my prayers.**
> *Together:*
> O Israel, trust in the Lord!

Leader and Family/Group alternate

(Family/Group in bold):

The Lord is gracious and just; our God is compassion-ate.

You have delivered my soul from death, my eyes from tears, my feet from stumbling.

How can we repay the Lord for all His kindness?

I will raise the cup of salvation and call upon the name of the Lord. All the days of my life I will walk in your presence. Thank you, Lord, for I am your servant.

We will bless the Lord

from this time forth forever.

The Lord is my strength and song,

and He is become my salvation.

I will give thanks to you,

for you have answered me.

Together:

And have become my salvation.

Leader and Family/Group alternate

(Family/Group in bold):

The stone which the builders rejected

is become the chief cornerstone.

This was indeed from the Lord,

it is marvelous in our eyes.

This is the day which the Lord has made.

Let us rejoice and be glad in it.

The Lord is God, and has given us light.

Blessed be the One that comes in the name of the Lord.

The Breath of Every Living Thing Shall Bless His Name

Leader:

To you alone we give thanks. Even if our mouths were filled with song as the sea, and our tongue with joyous singing like the multitude of its waves, and our lips with praise like the expanse of the sky, and our eyes shining like the sun and the moon, and our hands spread out like the eagles of heaven, and our feet swift like deer—we would still be unable to thank you enough, O Lord our God, and to bless your name, for even one of the thousands of thousands and myriads of myriads of miracles and wonders that you have done for our ancestors and for us.

Family/Group:

Praise the Lord, O my soul, and all that is within me, praise His holy name.

Leader:

Let us all drink the fourth cup, the Cup of Praise.

Elijah's Cup—The Cup of Hope

Leader:

Will the children please open the door.

At our table we have set an extra place. No one occupies the chair. Tradition says that this is for Elijah. The door is opened in hopes Elijah will arrive to announce that the Messiah has come. We remember the day Jesus took Peter, James, and John to a high mountain. There He was transfigured before them. His clothes became dazzling white! "And there appeared before them Elijah and Moses, who were talking with Jesus." Then a cloud appeared and a voice came from the cloud: "This is my Son whom I love. Listen to him!" (Mark 9:2–8, NIV).

Family/Group:

We praise and thank you, O Lord our God, for providing Elijah and Moses that day on the Mount of Transfiguration to verify and announce that all the years of waiting were over and that your promise to send a Savior, Messiah, had finally been fulfilled.

Leader:

Tonight we shared four cups, remembering the celebration of our deliverance in the past and our thankfulness in the present. This cup of Elijah focuses attention on the future. It is a symbol of hope for the Jews.

The Haggadah has challenged us: "In every generation, each person must view himself as if he personally went out from Egypt." Exodus 12:3 reminds us, "They are each one to take a lamb for themselves."

Family/Group:

But we know Messiah has come. We are free.

Leader:

Some people are not. By tasting the bitterness of bondage tonight, we share, we know, we feel their suffering.

Family/Group:

Our covenant, our eternal mission, is to share the Good News—tonight and forever. Our task is to take the Cup of Hope to all people. Jesus said, "Go into all the world and share the good news with everyone!" (Matt. 28:19, author's paraphrase).

Leader:

Will the children please close the door.

The Shank Bone and the Egg

Leader:

You will notice some items on the Seder plate have not been eaten. Jewish people, since the destruction of the temple, are unable to observe the Passover according to their understanding of the Law of Moses. That law said the Passover lamb was to be offered in the tabernacle where God placed His name. (See Deuteronomy 16:5; 1 Kings 9:3.)

God allowed the destruction of the only place where the Passover lamb could be offered because the Messiah, who was to take the place of the Passover lamb, has already come.

In the years that followed, the Jews provided a symbol of the Passover lamb by placing a shank bone from a roasted lamb on a plate. To it the rabbis have added an egg. This is to be a reminder of the *Hagigah* (Ha-gi-gah), which was the "voluntary peace offering" on the second day of Passover.

Family/Group:

We praise you, O Lord our God, for providing all of these symbols to lead us to your Son, Jesus. Through His death, symbolized by the shank bone, He voluntarily offered himself, making peace with God, reconciling us to Him.

As Christians, we recognize that sacrifice is no longer necessary. The offering of our Messiah satisfied this requirement. In His death there is life. In the shedding of His blood there is atonement for our sin. In Messiah's coming our Passover is completed.

Conclusion

Family/Group:

The Seder of Passover is now complete, even as our salvation is complete.

We were privileged to celebrate it this year. May we live to celebrate it again.

We praise you, O Lord, who dwells in our hearts, for our redemption. Speedily lead all people, redeemed, to Zion in joyful song.

Leader:

And they returned to Jerusalem with great joy and were continually in the temple praising God.

Family/Group:

NEXT YEAR IN JERUSALEM!

Recipe for Charoseth

Charoseth

1 apple, peeled, cored and finely chopped
½ cup walnuts, almonds, or pecans, finely chopped
½ tsp. sugar
½ tsp. cinnamon
1 tbsp. red wine or grape juice

Mix together the apple, nuts, sugar, and cinnamon. Add the liquid and mix thoroughly. Allow 1 tbsp. per serving. You don't need very much.

Suggested menu and recipes for Passover dinner

Note: An asterisk in a menu means a recipe will follow.

Seder Meal

Gefilte Fish* • Egg Soup* • Matzo Knaidlach*
Noodles * • Golden Yoich (p. 39) • Candied Carrots
Roast Lamb
Tossed Salad
Fresh Fruit Cup • Passover Cake*
Tea with Lemon

Egg Soup

1 hard-cooked egg per person
A pitcher of salt water (½ tsp. salt per 1 cup of water)
Serve 1 egg, shelled, in a small bowl to each person. Mash the egg with a fork and pour salt water over it according to individual taste.

Gefilte Fish Balls

3 lbs. whitefish, filleted	3 tbsp. matzo meal
salt and pepper	2 onions
2 eggs	3 carrots
½ cup cold water	

Grind or finely cut up the fillets into a bowl. Add the eggs, one at a time, then the water. Add the matzo meal, about 2 tsp. salt, and ⅛ tsp. pepper and blend together (setting aside the carrots and onions). Chill in the refrigerator for five to ten minutes. Then shape into balls of desired size.

To make broth for cooking the prepared fish, slice onions and carrots and arrange in a thick layer over the bottom of a large kettle. Season with salt and pepper. Cover with cold water, bring to a boil, and cook for about 5 minutes. Add prepared fish to boiling broth, placing them over the vegetables. Cover, again bring to boiling; then turn heat low and simmer gently for one hour. If necessary, add water from time to time to prevent pot from cooking dry. Adjust seasoning to taste with salt and pepper. Cool slightly before removing fish to platter. Serve hot or cold, garnished with the slices of carrot and the broth. If cold, the broth will be jellied. Serves six to eight.

Matzo Knaidlach (Matzo Ball Soup)

4 eggs, separated	1⅓ cup matzo meal
4 tbsp. chicken fat	1 tbsp. parsley, minced
1 cup hot broth	1 tsp. salt

Beat egg whites until stiff but not dry. Combine egg yolk,

chicken fat, and salt with the matzo meal. Pour hot broth over the matzo-meal mixture and blend together. Add parsley, if desired. Fold in the stiffly beaten whites. With wet hands, shape together into balls. These dumplings (halkes) are usually about the size of crab apples, although they may be made as small or as large as desired. Drop gently into about 3 quarts of boiling broth or salt water and cover tightly. Simmer for 20–30 minutes for small balls and about 35 minutes for the larger ones. Makes about 30.

Noodles with Poppy Seeds

8 oz. broad noodles
2 tbsp. poppy seeds

½ cup blanched almonds, slivered
2 tbsp. vegetable oil

Break the noodles into 2-inch pieces. Cook in a large amount of boiling salted water for 8 to 10 minutes, until tender but not too soft. Drain well. Toast poppy seeds with the slivered almonds in hot oil in a frying pan. Pour over noodles. Sprinkle with salt and pepper. Toss and serve very hot. Serves 6.

Passover Cake

Passover cake is another one of those delicious traditions. I make it only during this season, and the family looks forward to it as a special treat!

¾ cup whole almonds
1½ cup sugar
1¼ cup all-purpose flour
¼ tsp. salt
½ tsp. cinnamon

8 eggs, separated
⅓ cup sweet wine or sherry
⅓ cup orange juice
powdered sugar
whipping cream

Whirl almonds in blender until finely ground. Sift flour with salt and cinnamon into a bowl. Mix in the ground nuts. In a large bowl, beat egg whites with electric mixer until they hold short, distinct, moist-looking peaks; set aside. Using the same beaters, beat egg yolks until thick; then gradually beat in the sugar. Stir in wine and orange juice. Add yolk mixture to the flour mixture, folding until well blended. Add beaten whites and fold together gently and thoroughly.

Pour into an ungreased 9-or 10-inch-tube pan (with removable bottom). Bake in a 325° oven until the top springs back when touched lightly, about 1 hour. Invert the pan until completely cooled. Sprinkle with powdered sugar and serve with whipped cream.

Checklist for Passover Events

Palm Sunday

> Prop up a stuffed toy lamb on a bed of palm branches as a centerpiece for your table.
> Read related Scripture and have a discussion.

The Night Before Passover

> Search for the leaven.
> Read Scripture together and pray.

The Morning of Passover

> Burn the bag of bread.
> Share the meaning of this action.

The Evening of Passover

> Set the table with your best place settings.
> Place a copy of this book between every two places.
> Put a pillow on the chair where the leader will sit.
> Mother lights the candles before the service begins.
> The Kiddush—a blessing over a cup of wine or juice—sanctifies the occasion.
> Washing of hands takes place.
> Karpas—dip the greens into salt water and eat it.
> Break the middle loaf of three matzo loaves: hide half of it for the afikoman.

Tell the story of Passover following the text.

Bless the second cup, which is consumed at the end of this part.

Washing of hands before the symbolic meal.

Matzo—bless the bread before eating it. This is the upper piece and remaining part of the middle piece.

Eat a sandwich made from the bottom piece of matzo, bitter herbs, and charoseth.

Dinner is served.

After dinner, the Seder continues.

Let the children find the hidden piece of matzo, called the afikoman.

Grace after the meal is said over the third cup.

The fourth cup is poured and the Hallel is read responsively.

Drink the fourth cup.

Pour Elijah's cup. Have the children open the door.

Explain the shank bone and the egg that were not used.

Conclusion

You shall count fifty days to the day after the seventh sabbath; then you shall present a new grain offering to the Lord.

(Leviticus 23:16)

Chapter 3

The Omer

An "In-Between" Time

What Is the Omer? (Counting the Days)

"You shall bring in the sheaf of the first fruits of your harvest to the priest. And he shall wave the sheaf before the Lord for you to be accepted; on the day after the sabbath the priest shall wave it. . . . You shall count fifty days to the day after the seventh sabbath; then you shall present a new grain offering to the Lord" (Lev. 23:10–11, 16).

On the first day of the week following Passover, the cereal harvest began. The first grain to ripen of those sown in winter was the barley. An "omer" is a half gallon of barley. The sheaf was reverently cut and the barley removed, filling a bowl. Then it was taken to the temple in this symbolic way and presented to the Lord of the harvest as an expression of thankfulness. The counting of the omer began on this day. Wheat is the last cereal to ripen, and the first fruits from this harvest are offered seven weeks later.

When the children of Israel left Egypt after the first Passover and began their journey into the wilderness, God led them to Mount Sinai. Seven weeks later He gave them a set of laws to live by that would govern their relationships with Him and with each other.

Christ died at Passover time to deliver us from the *condemnation* of those laws. It was obvious we could never work hard enough to earn our own righteousness. Paul wrote, "My new life tells me to do right, but the old nature that is still inside me loves to sin. Oh, what a terrible predicament I'm in! Who will free me from my slavery to this deadly lower nature? Thank God! It has been done by Jesus Christ our Lord. He has set me free" (Rom. 7:24–25, TLB).

When God offered His Son as the perfect sacrifice, He did *not* mean we were free to go and do as we pleased. "Well, then, if we are saved by faith, does this mean that we no longer need to obey God's laws? Just the opposite! In fact, only when we trust Jesus can we truly obey him" (Rom. 3:31, TLB). "You see, the law itself was wholly right and good" (Rom. 7:12, TLB). The law is good—the trouble is with me. "It makes a lot of difference whether [we are] pleasing God and keeping God's commandments" (1 Cor. 7:19, TLB). Jesus kept perfectly the law of God. He said that the evil one "has no power over me, but I will freely do what the Father requires of me so that the world will know that I love the Father" (John 14:30–31, TLB). "When you obey me you are living in my love, just as I obey my Father and live in his love" (John 15:10, TLB). Obedience to God's commandments should be our normal way of life as we seek to honor and glorify Him. Christ has offered himself to do for us what we are unable to do on our own.

"On the morrow after the Sabbath" following Passover, as the first fruits of the barley harvest were being offered in the

Temple, Christ was "raised from the dead, the first fruits of those who are asleep" (1 Cor. 15:20). Fifty days later, while the followers of Jesus were gathered together celebrating the Festival of Pentecost (or Shavuoth), God gave them the gift of His Holy Spirit. The word to us today is: To those who obey Him, God gives the Holy Spirit (Acts 5:32). Those who loved Jesus and who were closest to Him felt His departure most severely. They must have waited with eager expectation for the fulfillment of God's promise, "I will pour out My Spirit on all mankind" (Joel 2:28; Acts 2:17). Among the last words that Jesus spoke before the Ascension were these, "And behold, I am sending forth the promise of My Father upon you" (Luke 24:49). The promise was fulfilled fifty days later as they became the first fruits of the Holy Spirit.

The "in between" time of counting the Omer allows us to prepare for this dual celebration: the event at Sinai when God gave Israel the Ten Commandments, and the event at Pentecost when God gave the Holy Spirit. Jeremiah 31:33 moves the original law from stone to human hearts. "I will put My law within them, and on their heart I will write it." Paul, writing to the Corinthians, said, "You are a letter of Christ, cared for by us, written not with ink, but with the Spirit of the living God, not on tablets of stone, but on tablets of human hearts" (2 Cor. 3:3).

Counting the Omer

What you will need:

1. chart (on next page)
2. barley
3. Bible

How to celebrate!

When our children are waiting for an exciting event they mark the calendar with a big X for each day that passes. When scientists are about to launch a space mission, they give a type of countdown, 10–9–8. . . . In the Hebrew tradition as the family looks forward to Shavuoth, they gather regularly for a "count-up." (See resource #1, below.)

Choose a convenient time for your family to be together every day. Count fifty days. Anticipate Shavuoth as though you are waiting for the visit of your very best friend. Celebrate it with *joy*, remembering the first day you met that friend!

Resources for Celebrating the Omer

1. *Chart for counting the fifty days*

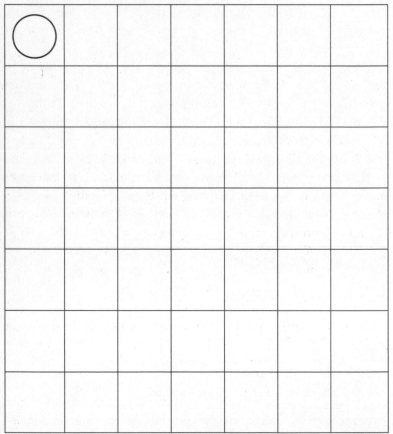

At the time of this writing, a one-pound bag of barley costs about 60¢. Buy a bag. Each day put a small amount of glue in the center of the next circle and place a "little barley in the bowl" as a way to count the days. Use the rest of the barley to make soup.

2. Counting the Omer—daily family service

Parent reads:

"From the day after the Sabbath . . . count off seven full weeks. Count off fifty days up to the day after the seventh Sabbath . . ." (Leviticus 23:15–16, NIV)

The whole family says:

This is the [first] day of the Omer. (Substitute the correct day as you count. For example: "This is the ninth day," making one week and two days of Omer.)

Read a portion from the Psalms (see next section—#3)
Record another day on your chart
Close with your own prayer, or the following:
We praise you, O Lord our God, King of the Universe, who has given us commandments to obey. It is our desire to be obedient to Your laws, knowing that they will enable us to live in a right relationship with You and with each other.

Thank You for picking us up when we stumble over stones and for sending Your Holy Spirit to comfort us!

3. Portions from the Psalms*

These portions from the Psalms are to be read each day as follows:

Day	Description	Psalm
1	The Law of the Lord	119:1–8
2	Obedience to the Law of the Lord	119:9–16

---

*The titles for these sections of Psalms are from the *Good News Bible* Old Testament: Copyright © American Bible Society 1976.

3	Happiness in the Law of the Lord	119:17–24
4	Determination to obey the Law of the Lord	119:25–32
5	A prayer for understanding	119:33–40
6	Trusting the Law of the Lord	119:41–48
7	Confidence in the Law of the Lord	119:49–56
8	Devotion to the Law of the Lord	119:57–64
9	The value of the Law of the Lord	119:65–72
10	The justice of the Law of the Lord	119:73–80
11	Prayer for deliverance	119:81–88
12	Faith in the Law of the Lord	119:89–96
13	Love for the Law of the Lord	119:97–104
14	Light from the Law of the Lord	119:105–112
15	Safety in the Law of the Lord	119:113–120
16	Obedience to the Law of the Lord	119:121–128
17	Desire to obey the Law of the Lord	119:129–136
18	The justice of the Law of the Lord	119:137–144
19	Prayer for deliverance	119:145–152
20	Plea for salvation	119:153–160
21	Dedication to the Law of the Lord	119:161–168
22	A prayer for help	119:169–176
23	True happiness	1:1–6
24	Confidence in the Lord	11:1–7
25	What God requires	15:1–5
26	The Law of the Lord	19:7–14
27	A prayer for guidance	25:4–10
28	Longing for God	63:1–8
29	A song of thanksgiving	67:1–7
30	God and His people	78:1–16
31	God and His people	78:17–31
32	God and His people	78:32–39
33	God and His people	78:40–55
34	God and His people	78:56–72
35	God the King	93:1–5
36	God the Judge	94:12–23

You shall observe the Feast of the Harvest
of the first fruits of your labors.
(Exodus 23:16)

Chapter 4

Shavuoth

Fifty Days Counted, Now Celebrate!

What Is Shavuoth?

The next Hebrew festival announced in the Old Testament and celebrated in the New Testament has a variety of names, each describing a part of its meaning and significance. It is not a man-made ceremony but God's Word, revealed for our understanding and blessing.

Seven weeks after the second day of Passover is the festival called Shavuoth, Feast of Weeks, or Pentecost. Shavuoth is the Hebrew word for "weeks." Pentecost is a Greek word which literally means "fiftieth day." In Old Testament times farmers brought their first-fruits offerings of barley to the Temple on the day after the Sabbath, at Passover. On that day the counting of the weeks began. Shavuoth celebrates the first fruits of the wheat harvest seven weeks later.

The instructions in Leviticus 23:15–17 say, "You shall also count for yourselves from the day after the sabbath, from the day when you brought in the sheaf of the wave offering; there shall be seven complete sabbaths. You shall count fifty days to the day after the seventh sabbath; then you shall present a new grain offering to the Lord. You shall bring in from your dwelling places two loaves of bread for a wave offering, made of two-tenths of a bushel; they shall be of a fine flour, baked with leaven as first fruits to the Lord."

Two more names identify the same event. An early command for this celebration is found in Exodus 23:16, 19: "You shall observe the Feast of the Harvest of the first fruits of your labors from what you sow in the field. . . . You shall bring the choice first fruits of your soil into the house of the Lord your God." Because of these instructions this festival became known as the "Feast of the Harvest" and the "Day of the First Fruits."

There is still another significance associated with this time in the late spring. It came to be recognized as a memorial to the revelation of the Torah, God's gift of the Ten Commandments at Mt. Sinai, on the fiftieth day after the Israelites were led out of Egypt (Exodus 19). Remembering the anniversary of the covenant between God and Israel, it is called the season of the giving to us of our Holy Torah.

God's timetable is remarkable. First He established His pattern for redemption in the death of the Sacrificial Lamb. As death visited the firstborn of all the homes in Egypt not covered by the blood, Israel was set free from her bondage. Passover is a memorial to freedom. Many years later, at Passover, Christ concluded that sacrifice, setting us free from sin and death. Paul identifies Him in the resurrection as "Christ the first fruits" (1 Cor. 15:23), for it was on the morning of the offering of the first fruits of the barley harvest that He rose from the dead.

Pentecost remembers God's message of law. "All that the Lord has spoken we will do!" (Ex. 19:8). Rabbis have said there is no liberty without divine law and self-discipline. A train needs rails. A river must have banks. Jesus didn't say, "Go and do what feels good." He said, "Go . . . and make disciples . . . teaching them to *observe* all that I commanded you" (Matt. 28:19–20).

Christ set us free from the law in granting us salvation. We could not achieve it. It is a gift to be accepted. Freedom always has two aspects. We are free "from" in order that we may be free "to." Christ sets us free from our own habits and actions in order that we may be free to obey. We become free to do not as we please but as God pleases. In a sense, we are set free from human traditions so that we may hear the authentic and complete Word of God. This freedom comes from the knowledge that it is no longer our own efforts, but it is God's power that is at work within us. This was then demonstrated and brought to completion in His season. Acts 2:1 says, "And when the day of Pentecost had come, they were all together in one place," celebrating this festival of the first fruits of the wheat harvest, "and they were all filled with the Holy Spirit" (Acts 2:4), becoming the "first fruits" of God's harvest. God's power came to dwell in us. The prophets were continually calling the nation of Israel back to the living God who had made Himself known at the Exodus. We can know that same God, through Christ, by the power of the Holy Spirit. In Acts 2 the Holy Spirit came at Pentecost to fulfill the prophecy of David (Acts 2:33–36) so that Christ would be recognized by Israel and known as the Son of the living God.

It is clear in both the Old and New Testaments that the Word of God often became weighted down and covered over with rules and traditions. Jesus said, "You invalidated the word of God for the sake of your tradition" (Matt. 15:6). Paul said, "You are slaves of the one whom you obey" (Rom. 6:16). How important it is for us to listen intently to the authentic voice of God in Scripture and not be hindered by acquired traditions and even prejudices.

"I will put My law within them, and on their heart I will

write it; and I will be their God, and they shall be My people" (Jer. 31:33). Remember and observe this festival with JOY!

In Old Testament times the twelve hours of the night were divided into three periods, or watches. Different men took turns guarding the city, each responsible for a section of the wall. The first watch was till midnight, the middle watch till 3:00 A.M., and the morning watch till 6:00 A.M. Since it is the custom to stay up the entire night of Shavuoth, studying and discussing God's Word, I have called it the Night Watch. It is a time for personal preparation, and traditionally involves studying a small section from every book of the Torah, signifying that it is *all* important. Just as the responsibility for watches in the night was rotated, let different family members be responsible to lead some of the activities, changing your watches throughout the night.

Shavuoth Friday

What you will need:

1. some special meals (pages 113–115)
2. the book of Ruth
3. an evening together called the Night Watch

How to celebrate!

Known as the Festival of First Fruits, these days celebrated a special time of thankfulness at the beginning of a new harvest. Although it specifically celebrated the wheat harvest, other crops were ripening, too. This is the day that begins the fruit harvest which ends on Sukkoth in the fall. The Talmud tells how the first fruits were to be gathered: "When a man comes down to his field and sees a ripe fig, or a perfect cluster of grapes or a beautiful pomegranate, he ties each with a red thread, saying, 'These are *bikkurim,* the first fruits for the Festival.'" Many families camped on the hills around the city the night before the gifts were offered. Symbolic meals were eaten.

On the day of the celebration carefully prepared presents were taken to the Temple. If you lived far away from Jerusalem, your offering would be your best dried fruits, olives, dates, and raisins. Those who lived nearby gathered fresh food from their harvest. Each family brought two loaves of their finest bread. Include some of these in your meal plans.

During the celebration it is traditional to read the book of Ruth. The story takes place in Bethlehem at harvest time and is therefore an appropriate Bible passage for the harvest celebration. We can trace the ancestry of Jesus and His birth in Bethlehem to this story (Ruth 4:11–17).

The Night Watch

What you will need:

A place for the family (choose a comfortable location that will allow you to be together without interruption)

A big box (or two) containing the following:

1. Bibles
2. the Night Watch schedule
3. pipe cleaners and/or clay
4. watercolors (and water) or little jars of Tempera, brushes, paper, paper towels
5. cheese and crackers
6. a chart that will help you locate stars (page 122)
7. Coffee cake (page 121), knife, hot water, instant hot drink mixes, spoons, cups
8. colored pencils, stained-glass window designs (page 124)
9. large pieces of paper, crayons
10. bowl of fresh fruit, paring knives
11. pencils
12. cottage cheese and sour cream dips and chips (page 123)
13. marbles

14. red yarn, string or thread
15. a simple family celebration (page 123)

How to celebrate!

We have discovered that this experience provides an excellent opportunity for developing and deepening relationships between family members. Generally most of us don't have (or don't take) time together like this. Sometimes as adults we go through these exercises with other adults in "small groups," trying to discover and get to know *other adults,* and all the while we are not known to our own family. We somehow miss the opportunity to allow family members this privilege. Instead of always building strong relationships outside of the family, I am convinced that some of the same principles should be applied to building stronger ties within the family. If we begin to deepen relationships in the basic unit God has ordained, this wholeness will naturally spill out into our relationships with other people, and both will be mutually supportive.

A good precedent has been set for "all night" Bible study and prayer. The psalmist said, "My eyes are awake through the night watches, that I may meditate on Your word" (Ps. 119:148 NKJV). Luke reports, "And it was at this time that He [Jesus] went off to the mountain to pray, and He spent the whole night in prayer to God" (Luke 6:12).

Choose a place where you can be close together. We set up a tent in the backyard. It is always our first "camp out" in the spring. A trailer or camper would be fun. It's different than just being in the house and much more exciting. You might consider visiting a local motel for an evening away; check in, have a swim, and then enjoy a very special family night. (This isn't necessary, however!) Take everything you will need to that spot so you won't be running all around, back and forth.

Look over the schedule. You will notice the selected readings are from many different places in the Bible. This is in keeping with the principle that it is *all* important. "All Scripture is inspired by God and profitable for teaching, for reproof, for correction, for training in righteousness; that the man of God may be adequate, equipped for every good work" (2 Tim. 3:16–17).

We realize that it may not be appropriate for all families to complete this schedule. You may want to use just part of the material. Sarah has a suggestion if you have young children: "Let them stay up for an extra hour or two past their regular bedtime." Remembering her early childhood, she thinks that would be special.

Resources for Celebrating Shavuoth

1. *Suggested menus and recipes for Shavuoth*

Shavuoth celebrates the Torah. Many verses tell us the Bible is as nutritious as milk and sweet as honey. For this reason festival foods include many cheese, milk, and honey recipes. After a long winter, the first fruits of the harvest will be especially appreciated. Include them in your menus.

NOTE: An asterisk in a menu means a recipe will follow.

Shavuoth Dinner

Fruit Cup*
Carrots • Black Olives • Celery
Baked Chicken • Garden Green Salad* • Vegetable
Challah (p. 39)
Baklava*
Coffee • Milk

Shavuoth Breakfast

Toasted Bagels • Honey and Butter
Eggs cooked your favorite way
Strawberries and Cream
Coffee • Milk

Shavuoth Lunch

Lox (smoked salmon) • Cream Cheese • Bagels
Honey Cookies • Fresh Fruit
Coffee • Milk

Fruit Cup

All over the world fruit soups are favorites for Shavuoth. They can be served hot or cold. The following is a recipe for a cold fruit cup:

1 qt. can grapefruit, cut	juice of one lemon
1 qt. can pineapple, cut	red grapes, halved
2 cans apricots, cut	4–5 oranges, cut
1 qt. can peaches, cut	juice of 4 limes
1 jar maraschino cherries,	1 lemon rind
halved	1 scant tsp. almond extract

Makes about 5 quarts. You may use fresh fruit.

Garden Green Salad

Try using only "greens" in this salad, combining vegetables that are available in your area: lettuce, spinach greens, cucumber, green pepper, avocados, etc. Finish it with your favorite dressing.

Baklava
Easy and Delicious!

Make syrup first and chill thoroughly!

Syrup:

3 cups sugar	1 cup water

Bring to a boil. Boil 10 minutes.
Remove from heat and add a few drops of lemon juice.
Chill in refrigerator

Filling mixture:
Chop (fine) 2 lbs. walnuts (or almonds)
Mix with 3 Tbsp. sugar and 2 tsp. cinnamon

Layer thin sheets of phyllo dough (1 lb. package) flat in a 9" x 13" baking pan, alternating with filling mixture
Cut into diamond shapes
Pour 1 lb. melted sweet butter (while still hot) over the top
Bake at 350° for 30 minutes until golden
Pour COLD syrup over HOT Baklava as it comes out of the oven.
Alternative recipe:
Buy one pound of frozen phyllo dough. Follow the recipe that is given on the box. This is a real *treat!*

2. Schedule for the Night Watch

Our family found it best to begin this celebration on the Friday night before Pentecost.

"My eyes are awake through the night watches, that I may meditate on your word" (Ps. 119:148 NKJV).

8:00 P.M. Discuss this verse:

"The fruit of the righteous is a tree of life" (Prov. 11:30).

What do you think it means? Hide it in your heart. (Suggestion: repeat it every hour on the hour to make sure it will be remembered.) Read the book of Ruth. If your children are small, this could be their bedtime story. It is very beautiful and appropriate to this season because of the harvest scenes.
9:00 P.M. Read, think, and talk about Matthew 18:1–4.
Each one in the family share:
My favorite childhood game
My favorite childhood hiding place
My favorite childhood pet
My favorite childhood person outside of my family

Discuss:

A. Qualities of childlikeness Jesus might have been referring to when He said this (example: simple, open trust)

B. Qualities of success in society that you believe the adult world stresses (example: rational, calculating, suspicious)

Model with pipe cleaners and/or clay impressions from your discussions.

10:00 P.M. and time for the first of a series of SLAP DOWNS (every hour take a few minutes for a slap down).

This is how it works. Extend your left arm out straight, and with your right hand starting at the shoulder, slap it, moving out to the finger tips and back. (Great for restoring circulation and that wide-awake feeling.) Change and follow the same directions reversing arms. Then work on your left leg. Don't forget the right leg. Repeat as many times as necessary to ensure staying awake until the next slap down!

Now it's time to *Paint a Proverb*. The following are suggested verses that relate to the meaning of this night. Read them, meditate on them, and then paint in your own way how your mind sees these words and share your results with the family.

Hear, my child, your father's instruction
and do not reject your mother's teaching (Prov. 1:8 NRSV).
My child, keep your father's commandment,
and do not forsake your mother's teaching;
Bind them on your heart always;
tie them around your neck.
When you walk, they will lead you;
when you lie down, they will watch over you;
and when you awake, they will talk with you.
For the commandment is a lamp and the teaching a light
(Prov. 6:20–23 NRSV).
My child, keep my words,
and store up my commandments with you;
keep my commandments and live,

keep my teaching as the apple of your eye;
bind them on your fingers,
write them on the tablet of your heart (Prov. 7:1–3 NRSV).
He who trusts in riches will fall,
But the righteous will flourish like the green leaf (Prov. 11:28).
The fruit of the righteous is a tree of life (Prov. 11:30).
The root of the righteous yields fruit (Prov. 12:12).
From the fruit of their words good persons eat good things (Prov. 13:2, NRSV).
Death and life are in the power of the tongue, And those who love it will eat its fruit (18:21).
He who tends the fig tree will eat its fruit;
And he who cares for his master will be honored (27:18).

10:45 P.M. Cheese and Crackers
11:00 P.M. Make a machine

Create a family machine in which each person becomes a part and a sound linking into the total group according to your design (pistons going up and down, gears going around, etc.). Don't leave out a wheel and remember to make your individual sound. The whole experience serves its purpose in just a few minutes of action.

Read Acts 2:1–13

1. *Describe the passage by each of the five senses.*

(Supply a word under each category):

a. sight (pick a color)

b. touch (a texture)

c. smell (an odor)

d. sound (a noise)

e. taste (a food)

2. *I feel as though the passage is a description of something that happened two thousand years ago and*

(choose one)—

a. can never happen again

b. should not happen again

c. should happen again and again

d. is happening again

3. The closest I have come to experiencing what is described in the passage is (finish the sentence)—

12:00 midnight It's time to slap down

A parent reads Genesis 15:5

Then take your family out under the stars and enjoy them together (God willing), thinking about Abraham and his descendants. With the "Stars of Spring" chart as your guide (see page 122), try to identify as many as you can, marking them off on your chart.

Spend some time thanking God for His creation.

12:45 A.M. Coffee and Coffee Cake (page 121)

1:00 A.M. Play "Partners" (Mirror reflections)

One person is himself. The other is his reflection in a mirror. The first person, moving slowly at first, must be followed by his reflection. After a minute or so, change positions.

Read some Psalms and color stained-glass window designs (with colored pencils) (see page 124). Perhaps take turns reading while the rest of the family creates designs (Ps. 1; 63:6–7; 42:8; 77:6; 16:7; 99:2; 119:18; 128:1–4; 119:62; 119:44–48; 119:55–56; 132:3–5).

Different men took turns guarding the city at night, each responsible for a section of the wall. The First Watch was till midnight, the Middle Watch till 3:00 A.M., the Morning Watch till 6:00 A.M. The civil day was from sunset one evening to sunset the next, because the *evening* and the morning were the first day (Gen. 1:5).

2:00 A.M. Slap down for a while—

Consider what Jesus said about "fruits"—

Matthew 3:8; 7:16

Mark 4:18–20

Luke 8:15

John 4:36

Read John 15
Without speaking, make a "Communal doodle."
Lay out a big piece of paper and provide some crayons. Create a meaningful group drawing of your impressions after hearing Jesus' words. . . .
2:45 A.M. Time for a "Fruit Break." A bowl of fresh fruit will really hit the spot.
3:00 A.M. The Imaginary Ball
A parent shapes an imaginary ball and throws it to someone. The person catching it reshapes it and throws it to another.

The beginnings . . .
Shavuoth is the anniversary of the giving of the Law (revelation on Mount Sinai). This is why we study God's Word, the Torah, all night. It is because we are thankful, but also because we want to know more of the Lord. We want to know and love the Torah.

Psalm 78.1–7

You shall celebrate:

Exodus 34:22; 23:16
Leviticus 23:10
Numbers 28:26
Deuteronomy 16:9–10
2 Chronicles 8.13

"Israel was holy to the Lord, the first of His harvest" (Jer. 2:3a). Some New Testament references concerning this festival: Acts 2:1–4; 20:16; 1 Corinthians 16:8; James 1:18; Hebrews 13:15–16.
4:00 A.M. It's time to slap down again—
Read Romans 8:1–4; Galatians 5:13–18
Mark each one of the above verses with at least one of these symbols:

⚲ = understand clearly
? = have questions about meaning
♡ = special inspiration
↘↙↗↖ = really personally convicted

As far as these verses are concerned:

1. What is the thing I must work on in my life?
2. In a word or two, state your need.
3. Name one thing you can do about it in the coming week.

Pray for each person in an area of need.

4:45 A.M. Sour cream and cottage cheese dips & chips (page 123)

5:00 A.M. Arm wrestle, followed by passing marbles with your toes.

If you can do this, you are still awake! Congratulations!

A study of *us* and God's first fruits:

"And this do, knowing the time, that it is already the hour for you to awaken from sleep; for now salvation is nearer to us than when we believed. The night is almost gone, and the day is at hand. Let us therefore lay aside the deeds of darkness and put on the armor of light" (Rom. 13:11–12).

Jesus said, "You will know them by their fruits" (Matt. 7:16a).
The fruit of the Spirit in us (Gal. 5:22–23).
Joined to Him to bear fruit for God (Rom. 7:4; Col. 1:6, 10).
What kind of fruit (James 3:18; 2 Cor. 9:10–11).

6:00 A.M.
Enter into a worship service of silence.

Sing together "Jesus in the Morning," or any appropriate chorus of your choosing. As the song ends enter into a period of silence. It is important to let God speak to us. Perhaps wander away for a short walk. Listen for a bell to call everyone back together again.

"It is good to give thanks to the Lord, And to sing praises to Your Name, O Most High; To declare Your lovingkindness in the morning, And Your faithfulness every night" (Ps. 92:1–2 NKJV). Now, anyone who would like to share should speak to the others, breaking the silence.

7:00 A.M. BREAKFAST!

8:00 A.M. Tie the red threads.

Harvest your first fruits.

Plant a fruit tree.

Several years ago we all went to a nursery, chose a cherry tree ($15.00), and planted it on Shavuoth. Richard dug the hole. After placing and straightening it, we prayed and dedicated our little tree to the Lord. The next year on the afternoon of Shavuoth, we tied red yarn around a branch that held our first green cherry. This year several branches had clusters of fruit and we chose the *best* one for the red ribbon. The children are expecting at least a *bushel* next year! They are also asking if we could plant an apple tree. . . . In case you are wondering, we *pick* our biggest and best ripe rhubarb stalk, tie a red ribbon around it, and take it to our first-fruits celebration. We tie red threads around special flowers or fruits in our yard that are *not ripe* yet, always remembering the principle: Our BEST belongs to the LORD.

3. Chart for locating stars (see next page)

4. Recipe for Coffee Cake

Coffee Cake (filling on p. 123)

¼ cup shortening	1 cup sugar
½ tsp. vanilla	2 eggs, well beaten
1½ cup flour	¼ tsp. salt
3 tsp. baking powder	1 cup milk

STARS AND CONSTELLATIONS FOR LATE MAY–EARLY JUNE AT 12 MIDNIGHT

To Use: Face north or south. Hold chart overhead. NORTH to north, EAST to east, WEST to west, SOUTH to south. To locate major stars start with URSA MAJOR (Big Dipper), follow heavy lines with arrows.

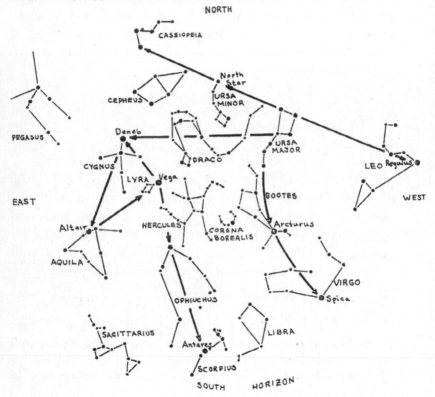

COMMON NAMES OF CONSTELLATIONS

Aquila–Eagle
Bootes–Hunter
Cassiopeia–Queen
Caphus–King
Corona Borealis–
    Northern Crown
Cygnus–Swan

Draco–Dragon
Hercules–Hercules
Leo–Leo
Libra–The Balance
Lyra–Harp
Ophiuchus–Serpent
    Bearer

Pegasus–Winged Horse
Sagittarius–Sagittarius
Scorpius–Scorpion
Ursa Major–Big Dipper
Ursa Minor–Little
    Dipper
Virgo–Virgin

Star chart drafted by: James W. Weber

Filling:

1 cup brown sugar	2 tbsp. margarine or butter
1 tbsp. flour	2 tsp. cinnamon
½ cup nuts	

Cream shortening and sugar. Add eggs, then dry ingredients, alternately with milk. Add vanilla. *Filling:* blend sugar and butter. Mix well and add other ingredients. Use one 8" x 8" pan. Put layer of dough, then filling, and repeat. Bake at 350° for 35–45 minutes.

5. Stained-glass window designs (see next page)
6. Recipe for cottage cheese dips

Cottage Cheese Dips

8 oz. cottage cheese
½ cup sour cream
salt to taste

Mix all of the above together. Then add any of the following to the desired taste and color: parsley, green onion, green pepper, paprika, pimento, black olives. Or add *all* of the following to make a flecked dip: slivers of pimento, green pepper, carrot, caraway seeds, and chives.

7. Festival of First Fruits Celebration (A service of *joy*)

Share this time with other families. Invite friends to join you. (Sunday afternoon works best for us.) The room or place of worship should be decorated with flowers, real ones if possible. If none are available, children love to make flowers. Let them help decorate. A yard or garden provides a beautiful setting for this festival. There should be a table set up where "first fruits" are placed as your friends arrive. This makes a wonderful addition to a Sunday morning Pentecost worship service. Greet them with these words:
"Enter in Peace"

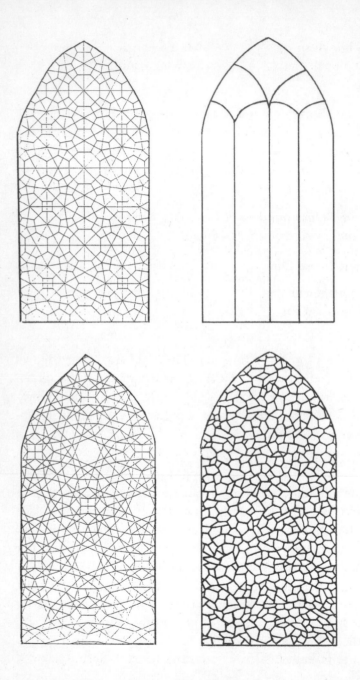

Introduction:

Briefly explain the celebration

Parents read verses (write them out on cards or have Bibles ready):

Psalm 119:105

Proverbs 23:15–16

Proverbs 23:24–25

Let a child read:

Ephesians 6:1–3

A parent responds:

Ephesians 6:4

Sharing time:

Let *each* family member "show and tell"

After the gift is presented, sing a response:

"I will praise You, Lord,
  with my whole heart;
I will tell of all
  Your wonderful works" (Ps. 9:1, NKJV),

A Key principle:

We offer God our Best!

Blessings and dedication:

Bless the gifts and those who brought them.

Dedicate the offerings to the Lord!

Remember, we are "blessed to be a blessing!"

At the close of the service after a time of visiting and refreshments (strawberries dipped in powdered sugar, lemonade, etc.), take your gift and *give* it to someone. In the days of the Temple, it would have been filled with good things. The Old Testament emphasis was on bringing offerings to the Temple storehouse. New Testament passages are concerned with giving to others.

Where we live, rhubarb and strawberries are getting ripe, but we don't limit first-fruits offerings to fruit. Spring flowers, a new sprout from a house plant, early vegetables, and home-made bread make appropriate gifts, too. One year a kitten was placed on the table. Another time Sarah's pet chicken, Ruth Ann, laid her first egg just before the festival. The egg was care-fully kept and presented as her special offering to the Lord. You will like the feelings that are produced as you deliver your gifts to a shut-in, neighbor, relative, needy family, or special friend.

Checklist for Shavuoth

Friday Night

Prepare a special dinner
Enjoy the Night Watch

Saturday

Breakfast
Tie the red thread
Harvest your first fruits
Plant a fruit tree as a memorial
Rest

Sunday Morning

Celebrate Pentecost, the birthday of the Church
Attend the service of your choice

Sunday Afternoon

Festival of "First Fruits" celebration

Now in the seventh month, on the first day of the month, you shall
also have a holy convocation, you shall do no laborious work.
It will be to you a day for blowing trumpets.
(Numbers 29:1)

Chapter 5

Rosh Hashanah
A Day of Blowing

What Is Rosh Hashanah?

The Hebrew word Rosh means "head" or "beginning." Hashanah means "the year." This name is used only once in the Old Testament. Ezekiel 40:1 says, ". . . at the beginning of the year . . ." The more common biblical name is "The Feast of Trumpets." This celebration of a new year is not in conflict with New Year's Day, January 1, which is our national holiday. Rather, it is intended to be a celebration marking a "spiritual" new year, a special time set apart for a new beginning with the Lord. It celebrates the Birthday of the World (see resource #1, page 135). The Hebrew calendar is very old. It is believed that the counting of years originated with creation. There are a number of ways to count the months. One system begins the counting in the spring. Each month opens with the appearance of a new moon. Every time there is a new moon, a new month begins. Hebrew festivals are calculated on this lunar calendar. In keeping with tradition it is fitting that the seventh month is holy, just as the seventh day has always been honored. Therefore, the calendar begins with the seventh month.

Hebrew Calendar

Name of month	*Number of month*
Tishri	7th
because the 7th month is holy, the spiritual new year begins with this month	
Heshvan	
Kislev	
Tevet	
Shevat	
Adar I	
Adar II	
Nisan (Passover)	1st
"In the first month, on the fourteenth day . . ." (Lev. 23:5)	
Iyar	2nd
Sivan	3rd
Tammuz	4th
Av	5th
Elul	6th

If you counted, you have noticed there are 13 months. The beginning of Tishri generally falls sometime in September.

Just as Friday is the day of preparation for the Sabbath each week, the sixth month, Elul, is to be spent in special preparation for the all-important seventh month, called Tishri. If you count the days from the beginning of Elul until the final day of this festival, they will number forty, called the Forty Days of Preparation. Use this excellent opportunity to show your children God's pattern in Scripture for forty-day time periods (see #2, pages 135–136).

In the Bible this day is called Yom Teruah, the Day of Sounding the Trumpet. "Speak to the sons of Israel, saying, 'In the seventh month on the first of the month, you shall have a rest, a reminder by blowing of trumpets, a holy convocation'" (Lev. 23:24). It is the beginning of ten days called the "High Holy Days," or "Days of Awe." Because of their meaning these days are also called Days of Repentance, Days of Admitting, Days of Returning. The observance concludes with Yom Kippur, the "Day of Atonement" (see chapter 6).

Three strands are braided together to give significance to this celebration. First, it is a day to honor the *kingship of God* and His authority over creation. "The heavens are telling the glory of God; they are a marvelous display of his craftsmanship. Day and night they keep on telling about God. Without a sound or word, silent in the skies, their message reaches out to all the world" (Ps. 19:1–3, TLD).

"Praise the Lord!
Praise God in His sanctuary;
Praise Him in His mighty expanse.
Praise Him for His mighty deeds,
Praise Him according to His excellent greatness.
Praise Him with trumpet sound" (Ps. 150:1–3).

If you have a globe, put a crown on it and use these symbols as visual aids for your family.

Psalm 19:7–11 (TLB) goes on to say, "God's laws are perfect. They protect us, make us wise, and give us joy and light. God's laws are pure, eternal, just. They are more desirable than gold. They are sweeter than honey dripping from a honeycomb. For they warn us away from harm and give success to those who obey them." Romans 3:23 reminds us that the King's rights and requirements have been violated: "for all have sinned and fall short of the glory of God." This, then, is the Day of Judgment when the worshipper appears before the Supreme Judge of all the earth. On New Year's Day we will all pass before Him like lambs. "The Lord looks from heaven; He sees all the sons of men; from His dwelling-place He looks out on all the inhabitants of the earth, He who fashions the hearts of them all, He who understands all their works" (Ps. 33:13–15). We know that God waits to forgive us *every* day. This day simply focuses our attention on repentance and provides a special opportunity or reminder of our *need* to repent. It gives us an opportunity to share with our children the principle of returning to the Lord.

Secondly, it is a *Day of Remembrance,* a time to consider one's place in the universe and one's personal part in the unfolding of God's plan for the world. It is a time when the past is recalled, memories are aroused, the future is envisioned, and personal inventories are taken. We are commanded many times in Scripture to "remember" the Lord and His marvelous works. This is also a time of bringing oneself into the remembrance of God that you might be remembered before Jehovah. Be especially careful to declare your acceptance of His words, "I am Jehovah your God." On Yom Hazikaron, this Day of Memorial, *everything* is to be remembered from the beginning. These two principles of remembrance are seen at the Cross. Just before He was sacrificed, Jesus said to His disciples, "Do these things, remembering Me." The thief who was next to Him on the Cross said, "Remember me when You join Your Father in Heaven." Place a goblet of wine or juice and a piece of bread on the table and remember. He has promised to remember you.

The third thread refers to the *revelation of God.* The sounding of the shofar is a symbolic signal to God's people that it is time for a spiritual awakening. Shofar is the Hebrew word for trumpet or horn, specifically a ram's horn. This instruction in the Old Testament to blow the ram's horn became a significant day of remembrance. It grew out of Genesis 22:13–14, and the account of Isaac spared, often referred to as the sacrifice of Isaac.

"Then Abraham raised his eyes and looked, and behold, behind him a ram caught in the thicket by his horns. . . . And Abraham called the name of that place 'The Lord Wll Provide.'" Because of this the shofar was blown to signify important occasions. As a communication device, messages were relayed across many miles. It was the signal every Friday to stop working as the Sabbath was about to begin. It was sounded at Mt. Sinai at the time of the giving of the Torah (Ex. 19:19). In this season it was blown to call Israel to repentance. At the sounding the following words were spoken, "You who are asleep, wake up! You who are in a trance, arise! Search your doings and repent; Remember your Creator . . ." (See resource # 3, pages 137–139). Paul seems to have alluded to this ceremony when he wrote, "And this do, knowing the time, that it is already the hour for you to awaken from sleep; for now salvation is nearer to us than when we believed" (Rom. 13:11). "For this reason it says, 'AWAKE, SLEEPER, AND ARISE FROM THE DEAD, AND CHRIST WILL SHINE ON YOU'" (Eph. 5:14).

The bend in the shofar represents a human heart in true repentance bowing before the Lord. At first we were amused to read that it was sounded as a means of getting God's attention, to be remembered and protected by Him (Num. 10:9–10). A year ago we were delighted to find one and purchase it. There is no sound in all the world quite like it. Now that we have heard it we would agree that it must certainly get God's attention! Symbolic of God's plan for salvation revealed in the ram's horn, cut a small bush or bundle of weeds and place a horn in the middle. Let this be another visual reminder on the table.

The first Hebrew letter of Rosh Hashanah is a ר (resh). It will take only a minute to get acquainted. Hebrew is read from right to left. Looking at the letter, be reminded that the past is closed. With the arrival of a new year the future is open. It also looks like a shofar, so be reminded to bend your heart before the Lord.

In the afternoon on Rosh Hashanah there is a special ceremony called Tashlich which means, "Thou shalt cast into the sea." At this time rocks, which are symbolic of our sins, are thrown into the sea and are then carried away by the moving water.

Rosh Hashanah

What you will need:

1. a horn or something to blow which makes noise
2. some symbolic foods
3. special family dinner (suggested menu and recipes on page 139–140)
4. the story of Abraham and Isaac (Gen. 22:1–14)

How to celebrate!

Rosh Hashanah is not just another day. It is distinctive in many ways. The table is set with your best, emphasizing the importance of the festival. Take a little extra time and invest in some family memories. They will accompany your children throughout life.

When dinner is ready on the evening of the Day of Blowing, let someone blow a horn as a means of gathering the family together. Read the ancient words that call us to wake up! Mother (or another leader) lights the candles as she prays. A parent (traditionally the father) leads in prayer in the ceremony of the cup and bread (chapter 1). An additional observance during this holiday involves a plate that is passed with apple slices surrounding a dish of honey. This is symbolic of the hope that the year will be a sweet one. It is customary for everyone to dip the apples in honey and enjoy this delicious taste treat. A special prayer of thankfulness is spoken by the father (or another leader). See resource #5 on page 141.

This meal combines traditional and symbolic foods. Be brave! It is customary to serve a fish cooked with its head. Traditionally this was placed in front of the father. You may choose to place it in front of the leader in your home. It also expresses the desire that for the coming year the head of your family will serve the Lord. This would be a *great* time for families to go fishing together! Or, save one in the freezer from your summer vacation fishing trip.

The Hebrew word for carrots also means "to increase." Therefore, they are eaten in abundance, symbolizing that God will increase our blessings as we walk with Him in the New Year.

Another tradition that we look forward to is tasting the first fruits from a new harvest. We refrain from eating one special kind of fruit until this night. I place it in a bowl on the table as our centerpiece. We have found it tastes especially good because we have waited for it. This makes us more thankful as we truly praise God for all the good things He gives us to enjoy. (See prayer on page 141, resource #6.) Where we live, pears and grapes are usually ripening. One year as we approached this day, I discovered that all the family members here and there had already eaten all of the common fruits that season. That week, at the market it was really fun to discover kiwi from Australia. I splurged and we all really enjoyed tasting this new fruit for the first time!

Instead of the usual twisted loaves of bread, the challah for this meal has a different shape. (Recipe found on page 39.) The loaf is round, symbolic of our desire for a full and round year. Save a little of the dough and form a ladder across the top. This shape symbolizes that we understand our prayers are directed to God on high. When we pray we are not just talking to each other but to Him. Birds with wings, made from extra dough and placed on top, symbolize our prayers flying to our Heavenly Father. Take time to explain the meaning of the symbolism to your family. If you don't have time to bake bread, buy a round loaf of bread for this celebration.

The account of Isaac in Genesis 22 is remarkably similar to

the sacrifice of Jesus. He was His father's only son; He was freely offered by His father; the wood for the sacrifice was carried on His shoulders, and the place of the sacrifice was on the hill in the land of Moriah which became Jerusalem. "Then Solomon began to build the house of the Lord in Jerusalem on Mount Moriah" (2 Chron. 3:1). When dinner is over and the grace has been said, read the story of Abraham and Isaac (Gen. 22:1–14). Talk about God's provision of a ram to be sacrificed in Isaac's place, a living picture of what was to come in His greater gift of Jesus.

Tashlich

What you will need:

1. clothes with pockets
2. some rocks or pebbles
3. a river or body of water
4. a Bible and simple service (found on pages 141–144)
5. refreshments

How to celebrate!

On the afternoon of Rosh Hashanah, it is traditional to go to a river or body of water for a special observance called Tashlich. This Hebrew word means "you shall cast into the seas." (We do this on a Sunday afternoon near the beginning of Rosh Hashanah, and several other families like to join us.) Wear clothes with pockets and pick up some stones or pebbles to fill them. After a simple family service, explanations and enlightening scripture, individually throw rocks into the water. Designate them for certain sins in your life for which you are sorry and are seeking God's forgiveness. This ceremony is in keeping with God's promise in Micah 7:19 NKJV, "You will cast all our sins into the depths of the sea." I have never known a child or grown-up child who didn't enjoy throwing pebbles into water. Flat ones are great for skipping! Getting rid of sin in your life is just as enjoyable! Know in your heart what sin the rock represents. Throw it out into the water. The first time I threw one into the swift and mighty Columbia River, I realized no matter how hard I might try, I would never be able to find that rock again!

See how far you can throw it. "As far as the east is from the west, so far has He removed our transgressions from us" (Ps. 103:12). A friend shared that as she reached into her pocket, her hand felt the smoothness of the special rocks she had collected. They were a group of small, well-polished pebbles, "Just like the sins of my life." One little girl looked in her pocket and said, "Oooh! This is a pretty one. I think I'll keep it!" How many times do we say, "I like this sin. I don't think I want to give it up just yet"? Another teaching for this time states that we are to go to a *fish-bearing* stream "as a reminder that a person is like a fish." We are just as likely to be trapped by sin as a fish is to be snagged or caught. Jesus, who knew the people around Galilee and their ways, also compared men to fish. He said, "Follow me, and I will make you fishers of men" (Matt. 4:19).

Resources for Celebrating Rosh Hashanah

1. Rosh Hashanah celebrates the birthday of the world

If you have young children, put candles on the Honey Cake and let this be a birthday party for the world. Talk about all of the ingredients it would take to make a proper cake. How big would it have to be? It would take all of the wheat from all of the wheat fields, all of the milk from all of the cows, all of the eggs from all of the chickens, etc. Don't forget the frosting! Let the stars be the candles on the giant birthday cake. Put on jackets and go outside together. Look up at all the little star candles and say "Happy Birthday" to the world. You will probably want to thank God, together, for creation.

2. Forty days—a period of preparation

The Solemn Season is a period of forty days, reserved for the purpose of personal contemplation and prayer. "Return, O

Israel, to the Lord your God, for you have stumbled because of your iniquity. Take words with you, and return to the Lord" (Hos. 14:1–2). It begins on the morning after the appearance of the new moon in the sixth month, Elul, and ends with Yom Kippur, the Day of Atonement. The shofar is blown, announcing to God's people their need to prepare themselves for the coming sacred time. "All the month of Elul before eating and sleeping let every man sit and look into his soul, and search his deeds, that he may make confession." This is a time for gentleness and personal reflection, a time to put things in order. Has a neighbor been offended? This is the time for a gesture of friendliness. Is there someone who has been neglected? This is the time for a telephone call. The sounding of the ram's horn was a reminder that the Great Holy Days were coming in one month. The blast was repeated every morning during Elul, with the exception of the Sabbath and the morning before Rosh Hashanah.

Our Lord set an example in His life as He was led by the Spirit into a time of fasting and preparation before He began His ministry among us. "Jesus was led up by the Spirit into the wilderness to be tempted by the devil. And after He had fasted forty days and forty nights . . ." (Matt. 4:1–2). There are a number of examples in Scripture of forty-day periods:

Moses on the mountain	Exodus 24:18; 34:28
	Deuteronomy 9:9; 10:10
Spies in Canaan	Numbers 13:25
Elijah in the wilderness	1 Kings 19:8
Jonah in Nineveh	Jonah 3:4–5
Jesus in the wilderness	Matthew 4:1–2
	Mark 1:13
	Luke 4:2

Watch for the new moon. Every night see it changing and be reminded that the Holy Days are coming!

3. Instructions for blowing the shofar (pronounced show-fer)

On the second day of the New Moon of the sixth month of Elul, the shofar announces to God's people their need to prepare themselves for the approaching time that is to be so special. This is repeated every morning during Elul and the first days of Tishri until Yom Kippur, with the exception of Sabbath mornings.

After the horn is blown the following words are spoken:

"Awake, you that are sleepy, and ponder your deeds; remember your Creator and go to Him for forgiveness. Don't be like those who miss reality in their hunt after shadows, and waste your years in seeking after vain things which can neither profit nor deliver. Look well to your souls and consider your deeds; let each one of you forsake his evil ways and thoughts, and return unto the Lord, so that He may have mercy on you."*

Forty days is a long time! I would suggest that you find something to blow, and let the children take turns, observing the *ten-day* tradition of the High Holy Days.

Starting on the morning of Rosh Hashanah:

1. Blow the horn
2. Read the words "Awake . . ." (listed above), until the observance of Yom Kippur
3. Read ten reasons for blowing the shofar (one each day)

The First Reason

Because this day is the beginning of creation, on which the Holy One, blessed be He, created the world and reigned over it. Just as it is with the kings at the start of their reign—trumpets and horns are blown in their presence to make it known and to let it be heard in every place—thus it is when we designate the

---

*From Mishneh Torah, by Moses Maimonides.

Creator, may He be blessed, as King on this day, for David said:

> "With trumpets and the sound of the horn shout joyfully before the King, the Lord" (Ps. 98:6).

The Second Reason

Because the day of the New Year is the first of the ten days of repentance, the shofar is sounded to warn:

> Whoever wants to repent—let him repent and turn to the Lord, the Creator.

The Third Reason

To remind us of Mount Sinai, as it is said:

> The sound of the trumpet grew louder and louder (Ex. 19:19) and that we should accept for ourselves the covenant that our ancestors accepted for themselves, as they said,
> "And that the Lord has spoken we will do, and we will be obedient!" (Ex. 24:7).

The Fourth Reason

To remind us of the words of the prophets that were compared to the sound of the shofar:

> "Then he who hears the sound of the trumpet and does not take warning, and a sword comes and takes him away. . . . But had he taken warning, he would have delivered his life" (Ezek. 33:4–5).

The Fifth Reason

To remind us of the destruction of the Temple and the sound of the battle cries of the enemies:

> "Because you have heard, O my soul, the sound of the trumpet, the alarm of war" (Jer. 4:19).

When we hear the sound of the shofar, we are reminded of His Temple.

The Sixth Reason

To remind us of the binding of Isaac. We should offer our lives to be sanctified through Christ, and thus we will be remembered by God.

The Seventh Reason

When we hear the blowing of the shofar, we will be fearful, and we will tremble, and we will humble ourselves before the Creator, for that is the nature of the shofar; it causes fear and trembling, as it is written:

> "If a trumpet is blown in a city, will not the people tremble?" (Amos 3:6).

The Eighth Reason

To recall the day of the great judgment and to be fearful of it:

> "Near is the great day of the Lord, near and coming very quickly. . . . A day of trumpet and battle cry . . ." (Zeph. 1:14–16).

The Ninth Reason

To remind us of the ingathering of the scattered ones of Israel, that we ardently desire:

> "It will come about also in that day that a great trumpet will be blown; and those who were perishing in the land of Assyria . . . will come and worship the Lord in the holy mountain at Jerusalem" (Isa. 27:13).

The Tenth Reason

To remind us of the resurrection of the dead:

> "All you inhabitants of the world and dwellers on earth, As soon as a standard is raised on the mountains, you will see it, and as soon as the trumpet is blown, you will hear it" (Isa. 18:3).

4. *Suggested menu and recipes for Rosh Hashanah*

NOTE: An asterisk in a menu means a recipe will follow.

Rosh Hashanah Dinner

Wine or Juice • Apples Dipped in Honey
Challah (page 39)
Green Beans • Whole Baked Salmon* • Carrots*
Sliced Tomatoes & Cucumbers
Honey Cake* • New Fresh Fruit

Whole Baked Salmon
(A Northwest favorite)

Grease a large shallow baking pan. In a saucepan melt:

¼ cup butter	¼ tsp. paprika
¼ tsp. salt	½ tbsp. Worcestershire sauce

Place the fish in the pan. Pour sauce over the top and spread on the inside of the fish, too. Sprinkle with ¼ cup grated onion or dried onion flakes. Bake at 350° for 30 minutes or more depending on the size of the fish.

Glazed Carrots

Wash, peel, and then slice carrots (about 8) into small amount of boiling, salted water. Simmer gently in covered pan about 15 minutes until nearly tender. Melt 2 tbsp. butter or margarine and 6 tbsp. light brown sugar in a skillet. Add carrots and cook over low heat until nicely glazed.

Two Honey Loaf Cakes

3½ cups flour	4 eggs
1 tsp. baking soda	2 tbsp. vegetable oil
2 tsp. baking powder	1 cup sugar
1 tsp. cinnamon	1 cup strong coffee
1 tsp. allspice	1¾ cup honey
a sprinkle of salt	

Bring the honey just to a boil in a saucepan. Cool and add the coffee. Beat the eggs until light, then add the oil, beating well to blend. Beat in the sugar gradually. Sift together the dry ingredients. Add them to the egg mixture alternately with the honey and coffee. Mix well. Pour batter into 2 greased 9½" x 5½" x 3" loaf pans. Bake in a moderate oven, 300°–325°, for about 1 hour. Cool in pans. Remove and frost. Prepare frosting by mixing confectioners' sugar with fruit juice. (I like orange flavor with this cake.) Make a mixture that will spread easily. These cakes are moist and keep well.

5. Dipping a piece of apple into the honey, a parent says:

May it be your will, O Lord our God, to renew a right spirit within us. If anyone is in Christ, he is a new creature; the old things passed away; new things have come. How sweet are your words to my taste, yes, sweeter than honey to my mouth. We should now walk in this newness of life. Grant us a year filled with blessings. (Ps. 51:10; 2 Cor. 5:17; Ps. 119:103; Rom. 6:4)

6. Prayer for the new fruit:

"We praise You, O Lord our God, King of the Universe, Creator of the fruit of the tree, who has kept us in life, preserved us, and enabled us to reach this season. Amen." (Add your own words of thankfulness.)

7. Tashlich Service

The participating families, parents and children, dressed in clothes with pockets, gather beside a stream to recite the Tashlich prayers. Sing "Down by the Riverside" or another appropriate song.

Gonna lay down my burden, down by the riverside
Gonna throw all my sins away, down by the riverside
Gonna know I'm forgiven, down by the riverside

Parents begin the service by taking turns reading Scriptures:

"Awaken from sleep; for now salvation is nearer to us

than when we believed. The night is almost gone, and the day is at hand. Let us therefore lay aside the deeds of darkness and put on the armor of light . . . the Lord Jesus Christ" (Rom. 13:11–14).

"Casting all your anxiety upon Him, because He cares for you" (1 Pet. 5:7).

"Cast your burden upon the Lord, and He will sustain you" (Ps. 55:22).

"You will cast all our sins into the depths of the sea" (Micah 7:19, NKJV).

"Then, with mighty power, God, exalted him to be a Prince and Savior, so that the people of Israel would have an opportunity for repentance, and for their sins to be forgiven" (Acts 5:31, TLB).

"So overflowing is his kindness towards us that he took away all our sins through the blood of his Son, by whom we are saved" (Eph. 1:7, TLB).

"I've blotted out your sins; they are gone like morning mist at noon! Oh, return to me, for I have paid the price to set you free" (Isa. 44:22, TLB).

"I, yes, I alone am he who blots away your sins for my own sake and will never think of them again" (Isa. 43:25, TLB).

Parent:	This afternoon the ceremony we are celebrating is called Tashlich.
Child:	What does that word mean?
Parent:	It is a Hebrew word that means, "You will cast."
Child:	On the afternoon of Rosh Hashanah why do we go to a stream of water containing fish?

Parent: It is to remind us that we are like so many fish caught unaware in the net of sin. This awareness should encourage us to ask for forgiveness. "Moreover, man does not know his time: like fish caught in a treacherous net, and birds trapped in a snare, so the sons of men are ensnared at an evil time when it suddenly falls on them" (Eccles. 9:12).

Child: What is the meaning of emptying the corners of our pockets after completing the Tashlich ceremony?

Parent: By emptying the dirt from our pockets, we remind ourselves that we should look inside and brush away every trace of evil so that we may become free from sins.

Child: Why do we shake our clothes or pockets?

Parent: Because sins are sticky! Sometimes they really cling and hang on. We should throw *all* of them away.

First reader: "Who is a God like You, Pardoning iniquity And passing over the transgression of the remnant of His heritage? He does not retain His anger forever, Because He delights in mercy. He will again have compassion on us, and will subdue our iniquities. You will cast all our sins into the depths of the sea" (Micah 7:18–19 NKJV).

Second reader: "In my distress I prayed to the Lord and he answered me and rescued me. He is for me! How can I be afraid? What can mere man do to me? The Lord is on my side, he will help me. Let those who hate me beware. It is better to trust the Lord than to put confidence in men. It is better to take refuge in him than in the mightiest king." (Ps. 118:5–9 TLB).

Third reader:	"O Lord, from the depths of despair I cry for your help: 'Hear me! Answer! Help me!' Lord, if you keep in mind our sins then who can ever get an answer to his prayers? But you forgive! What an awesome thing this is! That is why I wait expectantly, trusting God to help, for he has promised. I long for him more than sentinels long for the dawn. O Israel, hope in the Lord; for he is loving and kind, and comes to us with armloads of salvation. He himself shall ransom Israel from her slavery to sin" (Ps. 130, TLB).
Fourth reader:	"Our soul waits for the Lord; He is our help and our shield. For our heart shall rejoice in Him, because we have trusted in His holy name. Let Your mercy, O Lord, be upon us, just as we hope in You" (Ps. 33:20–22 NKJV).
Leader:	We came to the river this afternoon, our pockets filled with rocks. The rocks are symbolic of sins. As you reach into your pocket and feel a pebble, think about some sin, an action or thought for which you are sorry. Ask God to forgive you as you throw it into the moving stream. Know that He forgives you, that He is washing it away, and thank Him.

Allow for a short period of silent preparation. Begin to throw rocks into the river. After a few minutes gather in a circle for a closing prayer. Spread a picnic cloth and serve tea and honey cake.

Checklist for the Events of Rosh Hashanah

First Morning

Blow a horn

Read the words "Awake" . . .
Reason for blowing the horn
Continue blowing the horn every morning until Yom
    Kippur (except Sabbath)

First Evening

A special dinner
Include symbolic foods in your menu

Sunday Afternoon During the High Holy Days

Take your family to water (Invite some friends to join you)
Wear clothes with pockets
Gather stones in them
Follow the service for Tashlich

Remember this is a time for reflection and preparation. The
major emphasis in your family should be:

Remember your Creator
Go to Him for forgiveness
He will have mercy

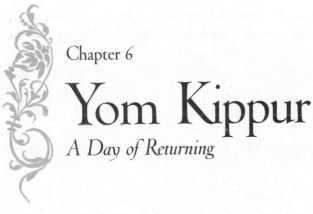

Chapter 6

Yom Kippur
A Day of Returning

What Is Yom Kippur?

Yom Kippur, meaning the Day of Atonement (at-one-ment with God), comes on the tenth day of Tishri. It is the climax of ten days of repentance. What was begun on Rosh Hashanah is about to be sealed. "Prepare to meet your God, O Israel" (Amos 4:12).

This is the day the worshipper stands before Almighty God. He confesses his mistakes and admits that he has sinned. It is his desire to bring himself into harmony with God. The point of this day forces me to recognize there is no way I can ever be perfect on my own. None of us can justify ourselves before Him. This is especially clear if I am endeavoring to keep the Law. "And the person who keeps every law of God, but makes one little slip, is just as guilty as the person who has broken every law there is" (James 2:10, TLB). "If we say that we have no sin, we are only fooling ourselves, and refusing to accept the truth. . . . If we claim we have not sinned, we are lying and calling God a liar, for he says we have sinned" (1 John 1:8, 10, TLB).

Job is a good example in the Old Testament of a man in need. In his hours of anguish he was painfully aware of his inadequacy to bridge the gap that exists between Holy God and imperfect man. "I cannot defend myself, for you are no mere man as I am . . . there is no umpire between us, no middle man, no mediator to bring us together" (Job 9:32–33 TLB).

God told Moses that this was how Israel was to approach Him once a year: "And this shall be a permanent statute for you: in the seventh month, on the tenth day of the month, you shall humble your souls, and not do any work, whether the native, or the alien who sojourns among you; you shall be clean from all your sins before the Lord. It is to be a sabbath of solemn rest for you, that you may humble your souls; it is a permanent statute. So the priest who is anointed and ordained to serve as priest in his father's place shall make atonement: he shall thus put on the linen garments, the holy garments, and make atonement for the holy sanctuary; and he shall make atonement for the tent of meeting and for the altar. He shall also make atonement for the priests and for all the people of the assembly. Now you shall have this as a permanent statute, to make atonement for the sons of Israel for all their sins once every year" (Lev. 16:29–34).

It indicates that even the priests weren't perfect; neither were the sacrifices. It was obvious that something was missing. The requirement had to be met year after year after year. It was never complete, never final. All that the animal sacrifice of the Old Testament could provide was a "temporary covering." This ritual was meant to be a symbol, pointing to something greater that was to be fulfilled in the future.

In the letter to the Hebrew people (which includes Gentile Christians, too, "Abraham's heirs according to promise!"—Gal. 3:29), it says, "He [Jesus] is, therefore, exactly the kind of High Priest we need; for he is holy and blameless, unstained by sin, undefiled by sinners, and to him has been given the place of honor in heaven. He never needs the daily blood of animal sacrifices, as other priests did, to cover over first their own sins and then the sins of the people; for he finished all sacrifices, once and for all, when he sacrificed himself on the cross. Under the old system, even the high priests were weak and sinful men who could not keep from doing wrong, but later God appointed by his oath his Son who is perfect forever" (Heb. 7:26–28, TLB). Continuing in the next chapter (Heb. 8:7–8, TLB), "The old agreement didn't even work. If it had, there would have been no need for another to replace it. But God himself found fault with the old one, for he said . . ." (at this point let's read exactly what the Old Testament said), " 'Behold, days are coming,' declares the Lord, 'when I will make a new covenant with the house of Israel and with the house of Judah, not like the covenant which I made with their fathers in the days I took them by the hand to bring them out of the land of Egypt. . . . But this is the covenant which I will make with the house of Israel. . . . I will put My law *within* them, and on their *heart* I will write it. . . . I will forgive their iniquity, and their sin I will remember no more' " (Jer. 31:31–34).

If the sacrifices under the old system had been enough, "the worshipers would have been cleansed once for all, and their feeling of guilt would be gone. But just the opposite happened: those yearly sacrifices reminded them of their disobedience and guilt instead of relieving their minds. For it is not possible for the blood of bulls and goats really to take away sins. That is why Christ said . . . , 'O God, the blood of bulls and goats cannot satisfy you, so you have made ready this body of mine for me to lay as a sacrifice upon your altar. You were not satisfied with the animal sacrifices, slain and burnt before you as offerings for sin. . . . ' After Christ said this . . . , he then added, 'Here I am. I have come to give my life.' He cancels the first system in favor of a far better one. Under this new plan we have been forgiven and made clean by Christ's dying for us once and for all. . . . For by that one offering he made forever perfect in the sight of God all those whom he is making holy. . . . Now, when sins have once been forever forgiven and forgotten, there is no need to offer more sacrifices to get rid of them. . . . Now we may walk right into the very Holy of Holies where God is, because of the blood of Jesus. This is the fresh, new, life-giving way which Christ has opened up . . . to let us into the holy presence of God. . . . Let us go right in, to God himself, with true hearts fully trusting him to receive us . . ." (Heb. 10:2–22, TLB). He has provided the perfect opportunity for us to be "at one" with Him.

I believe the principle of this day hasn't changed. What has changed is the way that has been provided for me to observe it. There will be a day of final judgment, and "if there is any person who will not humble himself on this same day, he shall be cut off" (Lev. 23:29). "And if anyone's name was not found written in the book of life, he was thrown into the lake of fire" (Rev. 20:15). According to Hebrew tradition, God is keeping good records. He offers to forgive us. The book is symbolically sealed on Yom Kippur, reminding us that one day it will be sealed forever. After the incident of the Golden Calf, when Moses came down from the mountain with the second set of tablets, he found the people fasting and repenting of their sin; and God forgave them. It was the 10th day of Tishri. "The Lord is near to all who call upon Him, to all who call upon Him in truth" (Ps. 145:18).

This is a single day in the year that has been set apart by God as special. It celebrates our "at-oneness" with Him. It was ordained in the Old Testament. How much greater is our reason to remember it now! Those whose names are written in the Lamb's book of life shall come in (Rev. 21:27).

What you will need:

1. a few minutes to bless your children (see page 154, resource #1)
2. large candle
3. an evening meal together (suggested menu and recipes found on pages 154–155)
4. 24 hours for fasting and prayer
5. story of Jonah
6. break-the-fast meal (see #3, page 155)
7. coin bank

How to celebrate!

Jesus liked to teach important truth by telling stories. One time He told a parable about two men standing before God. (I believe the story takes place on Yom Kippur.) One trusted in himself for righteousness or right living. The other man humbled himself and, unable to lift even so much as his eyes before God, asked for mercy. His prayer went something like this: O God, make atonement for me, the sinner. After the story, "they were bringing even their babies to Him in order that He might touch them . . ." (Luke 18:15).

It is customary in the Hebrew tradition for fathers and mothers to bless their children on the day before Yom Kippur. "Then some children were brought to Him so that He might lay His hands on them and pray" (Matt. 19:13). What a privilege—to lay your hands on your children, touch them, and bless them in Jesus' name. Take this opportunity to show your children how very much you love them.

Shortly before sundown, after blessing the children, there is a thoughtful custom of lighting a memorial candle in memory of a loved one who has passed away. We really miss my mother. In part, this book is in remembrance of her. A few healthy tears are always shed as we respectfully light this significant candle. It is a time to remember her life and love for our Lord. We let it burn throughout the day and observe the commandment, "Honor your father and your mother . . ." (Ex. 20:12).

The next twenty-four hours have been designated for fasting and prayer. I personally believe that fasting is a matter of the heart, and only you can decide if you want to enter into this memorial. It is customary that before Yom Kippur right relationships be re-established, personal problems be resolved and disputes settled with the people around you. Jesus taught this principle in the Lord's Prayer. "Your heavenly Father will forgive you if you forgive those who sin against you; but if you refuse to forgive them, he will not forgive you" (Matt. 6:14–15, TLB). We don't need to wait for this day to put things right with one another. However, just in case you have neglected a problem with another person, this day focuses attention and provides the extra incentive. Don't wait any longer! Take this opportunity and set an example for your children. Jesus goes on to say, "And now about fasting. When you fast, declining your food for a spiritual purpose, don't do it publicly. . . . But when you fast, put on festive clothing, so that no one will suspect you are hungry, except your Father who knows every secret. And he will reward you" (Matt. 6:16–18, TLB).

Fasting was an important part of life for many individuals in the Bible, from Moses to Paul and Barnabas. Our Lord, before He began His public ministry, fasted and prayed for forty days in the wilderness. If we look closely at Scripture we will notice that apparently Jesus assumed this would be a part of our life as believers. He said *"when* you fast," not *if* you fast. Three principles are linked together in His teaching found in Matthew 6:

"When you fast . . ."
"When you pray . . ."
"When you give . . ."

Fasting permits things of the spirit to be accented in our lives. It leads us to pray and share what we have with others.

"One man regards one day above another, another regards

every day alike. Let each man be fully convinced in his own mind. He who observes the day, observes it for the Lord, and he who eats, does so for the Lord, for he gives thanks to God; and he who eats not, for the Lord he does not eat, and gives thanks to God" (Rom. 14:5, 6). Consider this observance prayerfully, as a family. If you decide to fast, begin it with this thought: "But when Christ appeared as a high priest of the good things to come, He entered through the greater and more perfect tabernacle, not made with hands, that is to say, not of this creation; and not through the blood of goats and calves, but through His own blood, He entered the holy place once for all, having obtained eternal redemption" (Heb. 9:11–12).

Eat a preparation meal for the fast. Be careful not to serve highly seasoned foods that will make you thirsty. It is a festival dinner similar to Rosh Hashanah and Sabbath. Set the table with your best. Generally, just the members of your immediate family should be present. It is a personal time.

After dinner read the story of Jonah, who was sent to tell the people of Nineveh that they were going to be destroyed because of their sinfulness. In this story, which illustrates God's judgment of sin, Jonah tried to run away from God. Read this and remember: God is everywhere.

There are a variety of ways to experience fasting. Choose a pattern that fits your family and health needs.

The time of fasting ends as the sun goes down the following day. A light meal is eaten to break the fast and the day closes with words from the Psalm: "Let them give thanks to the Lord for His lovingkindness, and for His wonders to the sons of men! For He has satisfied the thirsty soul, and the hungry soul He has filled with what is good" (Ps. 107:8–9).

At this simple, breakfast-type meal, put some money at each person's place, an amount you would have spent on groceries for the day. Let each person put his share into a bank. Use these gifts to help needy people in an area where your family is particularly concerned.

At *last* it's time to start building your sukkah! After you have done this a few times, you will understand what I mean. We can hardly wait to celebrate Sukkoth. Turn to the next chapter for specific directions. You have five days to put it together. Tonight would be a good time to draw up your plans or choose a location. Have fun!

Resources for Celebrating Yom Kippur

1. Blessing the children

It is a Hebrew custom for fathers and mothers to bless their children on the day before Yom Kippur.

Place your hands gently on your child's head.

Pray specifically for your child, being aware of individual abilities and needs.

2. Suggested menu and recipes for family dinner on the evening of Yom Kippur

NOTE: An asterisk in a menu means a recipe will follow. Before the fast begins a special meal is eaten in preparation. Highly seasoned foods should be avoided so as not to cause thirst.

Kreplach*
Golden Yoich (page 40)
Boiled Chicken* • Baked Potato • Broccoli Spears
Tossed Salad with Light Dressing
Fruit • Tea

Kreplach
(Pockets of dough filled with meat)

In Jewish history meat symbolizes the stern judgment of God, while the dough symbolizes the mercy which accompanies God's justice. This is a traditional food served at Yom Kippur. It is still true that "mercy triumphs over judgment" (James 2:13).

The following recipe is a variation of the traditional Kreplach. It was given to me by a friend from Australia.

1 recipe pie crust mix	1 potato
1 lb. chopped beef (chuck)	1 turnip
1 onion	salt and pepper
1 carrot	

Grate the carrot, potato, and turnip. Combine with finely chopped onion. Add the beef and season *lightly* with salt and pepper. Mix thoroughly. Make pastry your favorite way. Roll until thin and cut into 5" circles. Fill half with meat mixture, allowing pastry circle to be folded and pinched together at the top. Brush the top with milk and prick in several places with a fork. Bake at 350° for 45 minutes or until golden brown. Serve hot with the soup course.

Boiled Chicken

Follow the recipe for Golden Yoich on page 40. Remove the chicken when it is fork-tender to be served as the meat course.

3. Suggested menu for breaking the fast

We enjoy a meal that is very much like breakfast.

Eggs • Orange Juice • Cheeses
Coffee Cakes • Coffee • Honey Cakes
Apples Dipped in Honey

Checklist for the Events During Yom Kippur

Just before dinner, parents bless the children
Light a memorial candle to burn during the day
Enjoy a festival dinner, served with your best
Read the story of Jonah
Pray and fast

Break the fast at dinner time 24 hours later
Read Psalms 107, 111, 145
Have a bank on the table; give gifts to the poor
Make plans for building your sukkah

*Another celebration, the Festival of Shelters, must be observed for seven
days at the end of the harvest season, after the grain is threshed and
the grapes have been pressed. This will be a happy time of
rejoicing together with your family.*
(Deuteronomy 16:13–14, TLB)

Chapter 7

Sukkoth
A Family Fort Festival

What Is Sukkoth?

Sukkoth was the first "stopping off" place for the Israelites
on their journey out of Egypt at the time of the Exodus. The
name is explained in Genesis 33:17: "And Jacob journeyed to
Succoth; and built for himself a house, and made booths for his
livestock, therefore the place is named Succoth." The Hebrew
word Sukkoth means "huts."

The biblical name for this celebration is the Feast of Tabernacles, or Festival of Booths. It is also called the Festival of
Ingathering. Three times during the year God commanded the
children of Israel to assemble in the Temple in Jerusalem. They
were to present offerings to the Lord at Passover, Shavuoth, and
Sukkoth. This is the third festival.

"On exactly the fifteenth day of the seventh month, when you have gathered in the crops of the land, you shall celebrate the feast of the Lord for seven days, with a rest on the first day and a rest on the eighth day. Now on the first day you shall take for yourselves the foliage of beautiful trees, palm branches and boughs of leafy trees and willows of the brook; and you shall rejoice before the Lord your God for seven days. You shall thus celebrate it as a feast to the Lord for seven days in the year. It shall be a perpetual statute throughout your generations; you shall celebrate it in the seventh month. You shall live in booths for seven days; all the native-born in Israel shall live in booths, so that your generations may know that I had the sons of Israel live in booths when I brought them out from the land of Egypt. I am the Lord your God" (Lev. 23:39–43).

Instituted in the beginning of Israel's history, Sukkoth was never forgotten. It was named as an observance in Solomon's reign (2 Chron. 8:13), and again in the time of Hezekiah (2 Chron. 31:3). The Exile interrupted the observance of the Feast, but after returning to their homeland the Israelites began the celebration again (Ezra 3:4). In Nehemiah 7:73–8:18 we read that all the people gathered as one man and asked Ezra the scribe to read the instructions from God's Word. Ezra opened the book in the sight of all the people and read, "translating to give the sense so that they understood the reading" (Neh. 8:8). The next day "the heads of fathers' households of all the people" gathered to gain insight into the meaning of the words. The result of their conference was to circulate a proclamation throughout all the cities saying the best way to understand this festival and command of the Lord is to *do* what it says: "Make booths, as it is written" (Neh. 8:15).

Our family applauds the wisdom of those early fathers, and we hereby recommend the same proclamation! "So the people went out . . . and made booths for themselves, each on his roof, and in their court. . . . And there was great rejoicing" (Neh. 8:16–17). Learning this way is so much fun!

One year Jesus risked His life to celebrate this festival (John 7). He was a "wanted man" in Judea. His family went on ahead and then He himself slipped quietly into Jerusalem. In the midst of the feast "Jesus went up into the temple and began to teach" (John 7:14). Everyone who heard Him marveled; how had this man become so learned?

The theme of His teaching related directly to the festival. "On the last day of the festival, the great day, while Jesus was standing there, he cried out, 'Let anyone who is thirsty, come to me, and let the one who believes in me drink. As the Scripture has said, "Out of the believer's heart shall flow rivers of living water"'" (John 7:37–38 NRSV). A special feature of this particular worship service was the sending of a priest to the Pool of Siloam with a golden pitcher to draw water which was poured into a bowl at the altar. With the approach of the rainy season, Israel depended on God to send rain for the next season's crops. This was a time for serious praying, asking God to open the gates of heaven and send the necessary rain. As the priest poured out the water, he visually demonstrated God's continuing and faithful love in sending rain. Like so many other traditions, it carried another deeper spiritual meaning. This was a demonstration or sign of Israel's hope for the coming of Messiah as they looked forward to the outpouring of the Holy Spirit which God had promised. Jesus, knowing the drought that existed in their hearts, probably quoted the familiar words of the prophet Isaiah, "Ho! Everyone who thirsts, come to the waters" (Isa. 55:1). "And the Lord will continually guide you, and satisfy your desire in scorched places . . . and you will be like a watered garden, and like a spring of water whose waters do not fail" (Isa. 58:11). "For I will pour out water on the thirsty land and streams on the dry ground; I will pour out My Spirit on your offspring, and My blessing on your descendants" (Isa. 44:3). The concluding remarks of the officers who listened to His teaching are significant: "He says such wonderful things! . . . We've never heard anything like it" (John 7:46, TLB).

At the conclusion of Sukkoth, on the ninth day, there is a special celebration called Simhat Torah. The name means "rejoicing in the Torah." But what is Torah? Volumes have been written in response to that question. Most modern translators use the word "law" to interpret the Hebrew word Torah, which occurs about 220 times in the Old Testament. In this celebration Torah literally means the Five Books of the Law of Moses, called the Pentateuch. These are the first five books of the Bible. It has been established that the word Torah means "to direct, to teach, to instruct." Similarly, the meanings "to guide" and "to show" help our understanding. Torah is painted in Hebrew picture form in the words "The Tree of Life." God the Father instructs His children, saying, "Keep My commandments and live . . ." (Prov. 4:4).

God was in the beginning. From the beginning He was seeking to make Himself known. The Bible as we know it is the record of how He made Himself known to people a long time ago. It is available to us today so we can know Him, too. Have you ever had a special celebration just because you were *glad* to have God's Word, the Bible?

Simhat Torah is not specifically commanded in Scripture, but long ago tradition gave it significance. There is an adage: "Turn the Torah, and turn it over again, for *everything* may be found in it." Affirming the truth that one must never stop studying God's Word, the last chapter of Deuteronomy followed by the first chapter of Genesis are read out loud before a gathering of the people. This action symbolizes the importance placed on reading the Bible every day. (See page 166—resource #1.)

Simhat Torah is a joyful celebration! All of the scrolls that contain the Torah are taken from the ark and carried in a colorful procession around the synagogue. Everyone participates in the parade, including the children who carry flags and banners decorated with appropriate symbols. Apples bearing lighted candles flicker brightly from the tops of the poles. The light from the candle symbolizes that we are enlightened because we know God's Word. "Thy word is a lamp to my feet and a light to my path" (Ps. 119:105). The apple reminds us of the verse, "Keep my commandments and live, and my teaching as the apple of your eye" (Prov. 7:2).

Bags of candy for the children add to their delight. This tradition is based on Psalm 19:8–10, "the commandments of the Lord . . . are sweeter than honey." Refreshments and house-to-house visiting conclude the afternoon. Each family returns to his own home for the final feast which closes the nine-day festival.

Sukkoth

What you will need:

1. a rough shack in your yard—see resource #2, page 166 (for a challenge, try making it without nails). If you are not able to build one—
   a. make a mobile of sukkoth symbols
   b. arrange a table decoration—resource #3, page 168
2. fruit and vegetables from the fall harvest to decorate your little hut
3. a pitcher of water
4. some special meals together—see pages 168–171, resource #4

How to celebrate!

Sukkoth is a special time set apart for living in a fanciful little house in your yard. The celebration centers in the sukkah. The significance of the festival is all wrapped up in the shaky little structure. As it is experienced its meaning is revealed. (See resource #5, page 171.)

The sukkah symbolizes several major principles.

1. It is a reminder that the children of Israel wandered in the wilderness, after the Lord led them out of Egypt, pitching tents or building temporary huts. The sukkah represents the faith they had in the Lord that He would take them safely to the promised land. When we sit in a sukkah, we declare our faith in God believing that just as He guided His children in that physical, earthly desert, delivering them to the land flowing with milk and honey, He will keep His promise to us and guide us to our permanent home in the promised land of heaven.

2. The booth is a reminder of the temporary endurance of material buildings as opposed to the permanent and abiding strength of our Lord and the heavenly shelter that He promises. "For we are sojourners before Thee, and tenants, as all our fathers were; our days on the earth are like a shadow . . . " (1 Chron. 29:15). If you have chosen to make a sukkah, here are some guidelines to follow. This should *not* be a strong, well-built, sturdy structure. It should be flimsy and shaky in order to symbolize this principle: "Abraham trusted God, and when God told him to leave home and go far away to another land which he promised to give him, Abraham obeyed. Away he went, not even knowing where he was going. And even when he reached God's promised land, he lived in tents like a mere visitor, as did Isaac and Jacob, to whom God gave the same promise. Abraham did this because he was confidently waiting for God to bring him to that strong heavenly city whose designer and builder is God" (Heb. 11:8–10, TLB). "For we know that if the earthly tent which is our house is torn down, we have a building from God, a house not made with hands, eternal in the heavens" (2 Cor. 5:1). The roof should be only lightly covered for stars, moon, sun and rain to filter through, a reminder that nothing can ever separate us from God's love (Rom. 8:38–39).

3. "When you have gathered in the crops of the land,

you shall celebrate the feast of the Lord for seven days" (Lev. 23:39). It was this verse in the Old Testament that caused the pilgrims at Plymouth to offer their thanks to God for the harvest. Our Thanksgiving Day celebration grew out of this festival. Fall fruits, sturdy vegetables and gourds make great decorations for the sukkah. Clusters of grapes, Indian corn, red and green peppers, small red and yellow apples are generally not too heavy to hang from the roof and walls. Baskets of colorful garden produce—eggplant, apples, squash, and pumpkins—help to make it attractive. In this setting be reminded of God's goodness and be thankful.

Another name for the celebration is the Festival of Ingathering. As you harvest crops or notice fall produce at the market, remember that they symbolize God's final harvest of His children. Jesus said to those who believe in Him, "There are many homes up there where my Father lives, and I am going to prepare them for your coming. When everything is ready, then I will come and get you, so that you can always be with me where I am" (John 14:2–3, TLB). Anticipate the time when we will sit with Him and feast with Him in heaven.

On the last night in your sukkah have a pitcher and water close by. Just as the pouring out of water at the altar signified Israel's dependence on God to send rain, let this experience be a reminder of the outpouring of the Holy Spirit upon us and be thankful. "No one can receive anything except what has been given from heaven" (John 3:27, NRSV). "For as the rain and the snow come down from heaven, and do not return there without watering the earth, and making it bear and sprout, and furnishing seed to the sower and bread to the eater; so shall My word be which goes forth from My mouth; it shall not return to Me empty, without accomplishing what I desire, and without succeeding in the matter for which I sent it" (Isa. 55:10–11). (See resources #6 & 7, page 172.)

Simhat Torah Party

What you will need:

1. an afternoon
2. Bibles
3. scrolls
4. flags and banners
5. a prayer shawl (white sheet or tablecloth)
6. sweet refreshments—candy for the children
7. a family feast

How to celebrate!

Regularly, by our actions, we tell our children what we think is important. We are "living proof" of what our hearts desire. Some friends of ours who have celebrated Simhat Torah with us join me in recommending a party as a great way to demonstrate for your children the important principle of daily Bible reading.

Sunday afternoon works best for us, about three o'clock. Because parties are a lot of fun with more people, we invite other families to join us in our backyard, asking each one to bring a Bible. Everyone gathers together in a circle and the reason for having the party is explained.

Begin with a blessing.

Then all of the members of the group join in a parade, singing Simhat Torah—see resource #8, page 173. Enthusiastic people help to make this a lot of fun! Fathers and mothers carry Bibles and scrolls. Children get to hold the flags and banners—see resource #9, page 174. (It's fun to carry a long stick with a burning candle perched on top!) The song is nice and long. When you finish the final chorus for *Z* reassemble in a circle, sitting on the ground. A call goes forth for all to witness the reading of the Bible. A parent is chosen to read Revelation 22. Another parent is honored to be the one to read Genesis 1. Let everyone join in saying, "There was evening and there was morning the first day," "the second day," etc., during this reading. Bring out the white prayer shawl (tablecloth). Gather all of the children together under it and let the parents surround them, holding this covering over their heads. Have different parents participate; one reads verses from Psalm 119 (see page 175, #10), another prays the blessing (#11, page 175). To close the service choose one parent to pronounce the benediction, a few words at a time, letting the children repeat it after the leader. (See #12 on page 176.)

Thirty years ago, with fear and trembling, I began to put on Simhat Torah parties for our church. The children that were blessed under the prayer shawl in those early years are now parents, missionaries, pastors, pastors' wives, worship leaders, and reponsible members of Christ's church around the world. In ways beyond our greatest dreams God has blessed those children through this simple observance.

I discovered this celebration crosses cultural boundaries. I took the Sukkoth celebration to Kenya to share with African Christians. Ten years later our African friends are still talking about the deep spiritual meanings they discovered in this experience. Every time I return to Kenya my African students remind me of the advances in their churches that began in our simple sukkah.

Serve refreshments from your sukkah—see #13 on page 176. If you live in an area where other families are using this guide book, conclude the afternoon with a "sukkah tour" or "sukkah open house." The children will especially enjoy sharing these with their friends. You might plan to have a "Sukkah Soup Supper" at the last booth on your tour. Some of our friends have suggested that our sukkah tour be a progressive dinner, which is lots of fun! If you are a single family observing this festival, a special conclusion would be a traditional Simhat Torah Dinner. (See resource #14 on page 177.)

The Bible is a "bestseller"! Take this opportunity to help your children get further acquainted with its contents.

Resources for Celebrating Sukkoth

1. Daily Bible reading plan for adults

Here is a plan which will lead you through the entire Bible in one year. See the Appendix.

2. How to build and enjoy a sukkah

Start building your sukkah as soon after Yom Kippur as possible. Traditionally, some part of it is put together just after the evening meal. You have five days to complete the project. This fort is not meant to be a super-structure; rather, it is a rough shack built by hand. One of the significant features is that each family builds its own little hut *together*. (I doubt if you could keep your children away!) If you can use the wall of your house or garage, the corner of a fence structure or hedge, do so! Improvising is the name of the game. You might use cement blocks with a bean pole or grape stake inserted to make a corner. For the sides use bedspreads, sheets, a drop cloth, plywood, cardboard (check with an appliance store for large packing boxes), or whatever you happen to have available. If a building is being torn down near you, ask for leftovers. Cloth on a wire track can serve as a doorway. (I use a red and white checked tablecloth.) Construct a simple lattice or trellis roof. Connect 1 x 2's or 1 x 1's and then lay rushes, grapevines, leafy branches, or pine boughs over the top. If you build your fort near a tree, the branches will form a natural covering. Lanterns or candles provide pleasant and adequate light. Be sure to make the sukkah large enough for all the family to be inside at the same time. We like to make ours large enough so that we have space to share it with friends.

Children are especially helpful when it's time to decorate. There are endless possibilities for materials. Here are a few suggestions just to get you started: posters, murals, flowers, Indian corn, fruit, vegetables and gourds. Sarah has made a small sign using the words of Revelation 3:20: "Behold, I stand at the door and knock; if any one hears My voice and opens the door, I will come in to him, and will dine with him, and he with Me." We hang it near the entrance. The first Hebrew letter in the word "Behold" is ה (hay). It is the sound of the breath of God. God says "I am" to us. Our response is "Here am I." As we offer ourselves to God we don't just say, "I'm here," but "I am present for you, Lord." This has become very meaningful to us as we enter our sukkah and invite Him to dine with us. We like to inscribe our booth "HOLY TO THE LORD" with a poster pinned on one wall. It helps us remember that we have dedicated all that we have and are as holy to the Lord (Zech. 14:20).

Remember, never make the sukkah *too* comfortable or sturdy. It should shake in the wind. Once you build it, use it! Eat meals there. We carry our picnic table inside *before* we put up the last wall. Invite friends and guests to enter and experience your sukkah, too. Our fall nights are generally pretty cold, so I remind friends who come for dinner to dress warmly. After considering the weather forecasts, we all try to sleep out in it at least one night. The children enjoy inviting a friend to spend the night (cats, quilts and sleeping bags help). When you are lying out under the night sky, seeing stars appear intermittently

between the branches of the roof, watch the leaves tremble in the wind and be reminded of the presence of the Holy Spirit. Reflect on all the lessons of the sukkah and know that you are recording memories that will last a lifetime!

3. Table decoration patterns

This activity is fun for the children even if you plan to build a sukkah in the yard. Let them make this for a centerpiece on the table where you eat your Sukkoth meals.

A. Small paper sukkah

1. take a brown paper lunch sack
2. cut off the rectangular bottom
3. cut the bag in half. You should now have 2 little houses (with no floors or ceilings)
4. draw windows and a doorway. These can either be cut or decorated with crayons or marking pens
5. take the bottom piece that you cut off. Fold it in half three times. Cut it like you would for a snowflake. Unfold it and lay it on top as the roof of your sukkah. Color to look like leaves and branches or gather small twigs and leaves to cover the top.

B. Lincoln Log Sukkah

Begin to build a log hut with four walls. Instead of making the roof out of solid materials, lay twigs and tiny branches with leaves over the top, weaving them together to give it a natural covering. Hang a little curtain at the doorway using scraps of material.

4. Suggested menus and recipes for Sukkoth

Sukkoth is like our Thanksgiving Day. The menu is similar to what you would serve then. An asterisk after an item means a recipe follows.

Fruit Cup
Roast Turkey • Stuffing • Creamed Onions
Relishes • Harvest Medley* • Cranberry Compote
Strudel • Nuts • Tea with Lemon

Harvest Medley

8 carrots, sliced
4 sweet potatoes, sliced
3 tart apples, sliced
½ cup brown sugar

salt and pepper
3 tbsp. margarine
1 cup water

Cook the carrots and sweet potatoes until tender. Drain. Pare, quarter, core and slice the apples. Alternate these in layers in a 2½-quart baking dish; season each layer with brown sugar, salt, pepper and margarine. Add water. Cover, bake in a moderate oven (350°) for 30 minutes, or until apples are tender. Remove cover and continue baking until top is a golden brown. Serve hot. Serves 6.

A Family Supper
(for a chilly evening in the sukkah)

Barley Beef Soup*
Garden Vegetable Salad Tray*
Challah and Honey Spread*
Hot Apple Delight*

Barley Beef Soup

This thick soup is easy to make and can be reheated when needed. Take it to the sukkah in a covered container to help keep it warm.

1 lb. beef stew meat
soup bone
3 quarts water
2 to 3 tsp. salt
dash of pepper

1 small onion
3 medium carrots, sliced
3 stalks celery, sliced
½ cup barley

optional additives:

1 can stewed tomatoes
1 peeled, diced turnip

Combine the first six ingredients. Bring to a boil, lower heat and simmer an hour. Remove the soup bone and add vegetables. Continue simmering until vegetables are tender. Season to taste.

Garden Vegetable Salad Tray

Fresh vegetables from the garden should be included in your Sukkoth meals. Tomatoes, cucumbers, peppers, carrots, and zucchini are usually available this time of year. Try this dressing in the center of the tray:

Raw Vegetable Dip

1 cup mayonnaise	⅛ tsp. curry powder
½ tbsp. lemon juice	½ tsp. Worcestershire sauce
⅛ tsp. salt	½ cup sour cream
¼ tsp. paprika	

Add finely chopped parsley, chives, and a little grated onion. Combine these ingredients and then fold in ½ cup sour cream.

Honey Spread

Milk and honey were part of the staple diet of the Hebrews from patriarchal times. It is not surprising that these two favorite foods were combined to describe Canaan, the land "flowing with milk and honey."

¾ cup honey
½ cup butter
½ tsp. cinnamon

Heat ingredients in saucepan until butter is melted and mixture is hot. Remove from stove and set aside to cool for best spreading consistency.

Hot Apple Delight

Arrange for this to come out of the oven just about dessert time. We love it served with vanilla ice cream.

5 to 6 apples	1 cup sugar
½ cup water	¾ cup flour
1 to 3 tsp. lemon juice	1 tsp. cinnamon
¼ lb. butter	

Quarter, peel, and core the apples. Slice them into a 9" square pan. Pour water combined with lemon juice over the apples. Mix the dry ingredients (I use a pastry blender) and spoon over the top. Bake for 1 hour in 350° oven.

5. Suggestions for your first evening in the sukkah

a. Before entering the sukkah for the first meal, gather the family together at the door and have a blessing:

"We praise you, O Lord our God, King of the Universe, who has instructed us to rejoice in this feast and gather together in this place. May we know your peace in the days ahead and be altogether joyful" (from Deut. 16:13–15)

b. Mother (or parent) lights the candles with the traditional blessing (see chapter 1)

c. Share the cup and bread with blessings (chapter 1)

d. Enjoy a special dinner

e. Talk about the sukkah and what important principles it pictures for us to learn

f. Remember the Grace of Thankfulness after the meal (chapter 1)

g. Read:
John 7:2, 10–19—Jesus observes the Feast
Hebrews 13:14—We are pilgrims living in temporary homes
John 14:1–7—Jesus promises to prepare a permanent

home for us in heaven

Hebrews 12:28—Let us be grateful for receiving a kingdom that cannot be shaken

6. Suggestions for the last evening in your sukkah

a. Enjoy a special meal together

b. Have a pitcher close by. After dinner let one of the children go and get some water in the pitcher and return it to the table.

c. Tell your children about the Temple custom during the Feast of Tabernacles, pouring water before the altar as a visual demonstration:

that they trusted God's continuing faithfulness and love toward people as He sent the rain

that they believed His promise to pour out His Spirit on them and on us

d. Symbolically pour out the pitcher of water on the ground

e. Close with prayer. As a suggestion to make this time more meaningful, encouraging participation from all of the family members, try "one word" prayers. Open with: "Heavenly Father, we are each one thankful for *all* of the blessings you shower upon us. . . ." (Let everyone name things for which he is thankful as he thinks of them. Don't be embarrassed if two people speak at the same time. God is able to sort it out and receive the praise.)

Close with: Help us to remember that You have invited us to come to You whenever we are thirsty and that You are the one who offers us the living water of life that gives us lasting peace through Jesus. Amen.

7. Scripture verses to read and discuss during Sukkoth (after breakfast, or during the evenings)

Old Testament

Leviticus 23:39–44

Deuteronomy 16:13–15
2 Chronicles 8:13 (observed during the reign of Solomon)
2 Chronicles 31:3 (observed during the reign of Hezekiah)
Ezra 3:4 (after the Exile)
Nehemiah 7:73; 8:1–13; 8:14–18 (after the Exile)
Isaiah 4:6; 44:3; 55:1; 58:11
Zechariah 14:16–21

New Testament

John 7 (Jesus celebrated this festival)
2 Corinthians 4:16–5:4
Hebrews 3:7–4:11; 8:1–2; 11:8–10; 12:26–29
2 Peter 1:12–14

Psalms 113–118 are to be read during these days. You might want to read a Psalm a day at a regular time that is convenient for your family.

8. Parade song
SIMHAT TORAH (suggested song for the parade)
(to the tune of "Are You Sleeping?")

Simhat Torah, Simhat Torah
Word of God, Word of God,
A is for the alphabet, *A* is for the alphabet
Praise the Lord, Praise the Lord.
B is for the Bible
C is for Creation
D is for King David
E is for the Exodus
F is for the first fruits
G is for the Gospels
H is for the Hebrews
I is for Isaac
J is for Jerusalem
K is for God's Kingdom

L is for the Lord's Day
M is for Messiah
N is for the New Moon
O is for our offerings
P is for the prophets
Q is for Queen Esther
R is for resurrection
S is for the sukkah
T is for the Torah
U is for unleavened bread
V is for the vineyard
W is for wandering, wandering in the wilderness
X stands for Christ
Y is for Yahweh
Z is for Mount Zion

9. *Patterns for felt banners*

These sketches are examples of how they might look.

Suggested materials: felt, glue, poles (dowels), apples, candles
Suggested symbols: tablet, crown, cross, star, Bible.
Suggested inscriptions: "Be Joyful," "Rejoice in God's Word"

The poles should have a cored apple on top, holding a lighted candle. This symbolizes, "We are enlightened because we know God's Word."

10. *Scripture: verses from Psalm 119,* THE MESSAGE

"By your words I can see where I'm going;
they throw a beam of light on my dark path.
I inherited your book on living; it's mine forever—what a gift!
And how happy it makes me!
I concentrate on doing exactly what you say—
I always have and always will.
You're my place of quiet retreat;
I wait for your Word to renew me.
Every word you give me is a miracle word—
how could I help but obey?
Break open your words, let the light shine out,
help me understand it so I can live to the fullest."

11. *Blessing under the prayer shawl*

We praise You, O Lord our God, King of the Universe, who has commanded us to teach our children about You. Bless them now as they stand in Your presence covered by the blessing of our prayers. We offer them to You today, praying that they will grow up with the eyes of their minds alert and eager to study Your Word. May the ears of their hearts always listen to Your instructions.

May our suggestions, loving discipline and example always direct them to You.

We offer this prayer in Jesus' name,
Your Word to us. Amen.

12. Benediction

(The leader speaks this slowly—phrase by phrase—so that the children may repeat the words, thus joining in the privilege of pronouncing the benediction):

The Lord bless you, and keep you;
The Lord make His face shine on you,
   and be gracious to you;
The Lord lift up His countenance on you
   And give you peace: Amen (Num. 6:24–25).

13. Refreshments for Simhat Torah party

Fluden* • Strudel • Apples
Grapes • Nuts • Punch

Hot water for tea, coffee, hot chocolate

Fluden

Pastry	Filling 1	Filling 2
3 cups flour	¼ cup apricot jam	¼ cup apricot jam
1 cup margarine or butter	1 cup dates, chopped	2 to 3 tart apples (core, peel, & slice)
1 cup sugar	1 cup nuts, chopped	
2 eggs	1 tsp. cinnamon	⅓ cup brown sugar
1 tbsp. water	1 tbsp. orange juice	juice of one lemon

Combine flour, margarine, and sugar in a bowl. Add eggs and water to make dough. Divide in three sections. Press one-third of the dough to cover the bottom and sides of a well greased 11" x 7" x 3" pan. Spread jam over pastry and sprinkle with Filling 1. Sprinkle second section of dough, covering first layer. Spread it with jam and sprinkle with Filling 2. Sprinkle third section of dough over the top. Press down. Beat an egg white and spread it over the top. Then sprinkle with sugar. Bake at 300°—325° for 1½ hours.

Decorate the fluden with white flowers to symbolize the purity of God's Word. I found these instructions in a book early one fall as I was preparing ahead for Simhat Torah. Imagine our surprise and blessing when we discovered one white Easter Lily blooming in our yard in October in Washington State, just in time for this celebration. Needless to say, our fluden that year was decorated with a very special white flower!

14. Menu and recipes for Simhat Torah dinner

NOTE: An asterisk in a menu means a recipe will follow.

Golden Yoich (see page 39) • Rolls*
Corn • Stuffed Cabbage Leaves* • Beets
Sponge Cake • Nuts • Fresh Fruit Balls
Tea with Lemon

Our children can hardly wait for Sukkoth every year. One major reason is this traditional and favorite food that I always make at least once during sukkah season.

Stuffed Cabbage Leaves

1 head cabbage (steam over boiling water until the leaves are pliable enough to roll)
1 pound ground beef
1 medium onion, chopped
1 tsp. salt
dash pepper
½ cup cooked rice or bread crumbs (or your favorite meat-loaf filler)
1 egg, slightly beaten

Mix these ingredients together and place a spoonful of the filling on a leaf. Roll up and tuck in the edges. Place in a greased 2-quart casserole dish. Continue tucking them in until all of the filling is used.

Combine:

2 cups tomato juice
2 tbsp. vinegar
2 tbsp. brown sugar
1 bay leaf

Pour over the top and bake, covered, at 350° for about one hour.

Rolls

Make little rolls from Challah dough (recipe, page 39). Spread the tops with an egg-and-water mixture. Then sprinkle with sesame seeds, poppy seeds, or coarse salt and chopped onion. Let rise on greased baking sheet. Bake at 350° about 15 minutes.

Checklist for Sukkoth

Begin to build a sukkah on the evening of Yom Kippur

First Night of Sukkoth

Before entering the sukkah for your first meal, pause at the door and pray together, dedicating it to the Lord
Enjoy a special dinner together

Things to Do in Your Sukkah

Invite friends to join you
Eat breakfast there
Sleep out one night, if possible
Read and discuss suggested Scripture passages

Last Night of Sukkoth

After dinner demonstrate with a pitcher of water (John 7)
Discuss the meaning of God's outpouring of the Holy Spirit

Sunday Afternoon During Sukkoth

Enjoy a Simhat Torah Party
This is a good time to begin daily Bible reading

A Last Word

One of the major messages circulating in the media today concerns the family. What we are experiencing is a *reaction* to the stress and pressures that are damaging this cherished institution and a *desire* among many to rediscover its significance. Obviously, good family life doesn't just happen. It takes understanding, careful attention, and intentional choosing to make it work!

Notice first that nearly every society recorded in history has had at its center the family. Next, it should be remembered that deeply rooted and central to many cultures is the table around which the family gathers. For our example we have looked specifically at the Hebrew tradition. In his book *The Recovery of Family Life*, Elton Trueblood says, "All who know anything about the Jewish religion are aware of the power that lies in the special Jewish home celebrations, especially at the beginning of the Sabbath on Friday nights."[1] The child who participates in this regular event senses that he belongs to an ongoing tradition that has deep significance. Psychologists tell us that traditions build feelings of security into children, enabling them to "cope" as adults. Relationships grow as people experience things together. The family festivals have played an important part in unifying God's people throughout the centuries in both joy and persecution. No outside force has ever been able to stop

---

[1] Elton Trueblood, *The Recovery of Family Life* (New York: Harper & Bros., 1953), p. 121.

prayer around the table in a private home at sundown on Friday night.

Jesus taught that His Father's desire for us was not a religion but *life*. We have often heard it said that the church is not the building but the *people*. "If we can believe that a home is potentially as much a sanctuary as any ecclesiastical building can ever be, we are well on the way to the recovery of family life which our generation so sorely needs."[2]

Trueblood goes on to say, "Each home will have to make its own experiment in religious education if the moral sag of our time is to be altered. . . . The best education is that of the laboratory and the only laboratory in which the most important lessons can be learned is that of the . . . home."[3]

Promoting that statement, secular teachers and religious educators tell us that of what they do, most of the value depends on how much they are being supported by the home from which the child comes—and to which he returns! "Fortunately, we do not need to choose between religion in the church and religion in the home, since both work together easily, but if choice were necessary, it is *clear* where the priority would be."[4]

Give it your careful attention.

All of this may seem new and somewhat overwhelming. Don't let that discourage you. We have found that every time we *try*, we learn something new. God blesses even an attempt! Use the checklists provided at the end of the chapters. One friend says he makes up 3"x 5" cue cards and has them beside his place at the table. Another friend says she doesn't try any new recipes the first time at one of the festivals. For her it is enough managing a new routine. Remember, we are not observing "the letter of the law" but the spirit behind the instructions. We hope that you will intentionally choose to try!

It is psychologically true in relationships that "doing things

---

[2]Ibid., p. 120.
[3]Ibid., p. 125.
[4]Ibid., p. 113.

for the one you love enriches your love for that one." Observing these biblical feasts is one way to acknowledge and demonstrate your love for the Lord. At the same time, all of these activities are speaking volumes to your children. Memories are being written on their hearts.

> And these words, which I am commanding *you* today, shall be on *your* heart; and you shall teach them diligently to your children . . . (Deut. 6:6–7).
>
> Our children too shall serve Him, for they shall hear from us about the wonders of the Lord; generations yet unborn shall hear of all the miracles He did for us (Ps. 22:30–31 TLB).

Special Helps

Calendar for Celebrating Biblical Feasts

So teach us to number our days, that we may apply our
hearts unto wisdom. Psalm 90:12, KJV

	2004	2005	2006	2007	2008	2009	2010	2011
Passover	Apr. 8	Mar. 24	Apr. 13	Apr. 5	Mar. 20	Apr. 9	Apr. 1	Apr. 21
Shavuoth	May 30	May 15	June 4	May 27	May 11	May 31	May 23	June 8
Rosh Hashanah	Sep. 16	Oct. 4	Sep. 23	Sep. 13	Sep. 30	Sep. 19	Sep. 9	Sep. 29
Yom Kippur	Sep. 25	Oct. 13	Oct. 2	Sep. 22	Oct. 9	Sep. 28	Sep. 18	Oct. 8
Sukkoth	Sep. 30	Oct. 18	Oct. 7	Sep. 27	Oct. 14	Oct. 3	Sep. 23	Oct. 13

This calendar is based on the Hebrew Calendar with adjustments for Christian Holy Days.

Sabbath begins at sundown on Friday night and ends when the first three stars appear in the evening sky on Saturday.

Celebrate the Seasons of God's Year

<table>
<tr><td>*LEVITICUS 23*
Cycle of the week</td><td>NEW TESTAMENT
Cycle of history</td></tr>
</table>

	Sabbath				"Christ"	
Get ready	Fri	Sun	*Remember*	Old Testament		New Testament
to	Thurs	Mon	*its glory*	*Get ready to*		*Do this in*
observe	Wed	Tues		*observe*		*Remembrance*

Spring

Cycle of the year		*Cycle of History*
The LORD'S PASSOVER	Wine—His Blood	Sacrifice of CHRIST THE LAMB
Feast of Unleavened Bread	Bread—His Body	He was without sin
First Fruits—Barley Harvest	"on the day after the Sabbath"	Resurrection—Christ the "first fruits" of the dead (1 Cor. 15:20)
Count fifty days		Count fifty days
First Fruits—Wheat Harvest	Shavuoth—Pentecost	First Fruits of the Holy Spirit (Acts 2:1–4)

Summer

"Now learn this parable *from the fig tree:* when its branch has already become tender, and puts forth its leaves, you know that summer is near; even so you too, when you see all these things, recognize that He is near, right at the door" (Matt. 24:32–33).

Fall

Cycle of the year		*Cycle of History*
Blowing of Trumpets	Rosh Hashanah	The coming of the *Son of Man with a great trumpet* (Matt. 24:30–31)

Day of Atonement	Yom Kippur	The hour of God's Judgment and the Lamb's Book of Life
Feast of Booths	Sukkoth	Heaven
Gather in the crops		The final harvest of God's people

"There remains therefore a Sabbath rest for the people of God" (Heb. 4:9). "Christ has already entered there. He is resting from his work, just as God did after the creation. Let us do our best to go into that place of rest too, being careful not to disobey God. . . . Jesus the Son of God is our great High Priest who has gone to heaven itself to help us; therefore let us never stop trusting him" (Heb. 9:10–14).

Appendix

Bible Reading Plan[1]

JANUARY
Book & Chapter
1 Gen. 1–3
2 Gen. 4–6
3 Gen. 7–9
4 Gen. 10–12
5 Gen. 13–15
6 Gen. 16–18
7 Gen. 19–22
8 Job 1–3
9 Job 4–6
10 Job 7–9
11 Job 10–12
12 Job 13–15
13 Job 16–18
14 Job 19–21
15 Job 22–24
16 Job 25–27
17 Job 28–30
18 Job 31–33
19 Job 34–36
20 Job 37–39
21 Job 40–42
22 Gen. 23–25
23 Gen. 26–28
24 Gen. 29–31
25 Gen. 32–34
26 Gen. 35–37
27 Gen. 38–40
28 Gen. 41–43
29 Gen. 44–46
30 Gen. 47–49
31 Gen. 50; Ex. 1,2

FEBRUARY
Book & Chapter
1 Ex. 3–5
2 Ex. 6–8
3 Ex. 9–11
4 Ex. 12–14
5 Ex. 15–17
6 Ex. 18–20
7 Ex. 21–23
8 Ex. 24–26
9 Ex. 27–29
10 Ex. 30–32
11 Ex. 33–35
12 Ex. 36–38
13 Ex. 39,40; Psalm 90
14 Lev. 1–3
15 Lev. 4–6
16 Lev. 7–9
17 Lev. 10–12
18 Lev. 13–15
19 Lev. 16–18
20 Lev. 19–21
21 Lev. 22–24
22 Lev. 25–27
23 Num. 1–3
24 Num. 4–6
25 Num. 7–9
26 Num. 10–12
27 Num. 13–15
28 Num. 16–18

MARCH
Book & Chapter
1 Num. 19–21
2 Num. 22–24
3 Num. 25–27
4 Num. 28–30
5 Num. 31–33
6 Num. 34–36
7 Deut. 1–3
8 Deut. 4–6
9 Deut. 7–9
10 Deut. 10–12
11 Deut. 13–15
12 Deut. 16–18
13 Deut. 19–21
14 Deut. 22–24
15 Deut. 25–27
16 Deut. 28–30
17 Deut. 31–34
18 Psalm 91, Joshua 1–3
19 Joshua 4–6

20 Joshua 7–9
21 Joshua 10–12
22 Joshua 13–15
23 Joshua 16–18
24 Joshua 19–21
25 Joshua 22–24
26 Judges 1–3
27 Judges 4–6
28 Judges 7–9
29 Judges 10–12
30 Judges 13–15
31 Judges 16–18

APRIL
Book & Chapter

1 Judges 19–21
2 Ruth 1–4
3 1 Sam. 1–3
4 1 Sam. 4–6
5 1 Sam. 7–9
6 1 Sam. 10–12
7 1 Sam. 13:1—
16:13; Psalm 23
8 1 Sam. 16:14—
19:11; Psalm 59
9 1 Sam. 19:12—
21:15; Psalms 34,
56
10 1 Sam. 22:1, 2;
Psalms 57, 142
11 1 Sam. 22:3–23;
Psalm 52
12 1 Sam. 23; Psalms
54, 63
13 1 Sam. 24–26
14 1 Sam. 27–29
15 1 Sam. 30, 31; 2
Sam. 1
16 2 Sam. 2–4
17 2 Sam. 5–7; Psalm
30

18 2 Sam. 8–10; Psalm
60
19 2 Sam. 11:1—
12:14; Psalms 51,
32
20 2 Sam. 12:15—
15:37
21 2 Sam. 16; Psalms
3, 69
22 2 Sam. 17–19
23 2 Sam. 20–22;
Psalm 64
24 2 Sam. 23, 24;
Psalms 70, 18
25 Psalms 4–8
26 Psalms 9, 11–17
27 Psalms 19–22
28 Psalms 24–28
29 Psalms 29, 31, 35
30 Psalms 36–39

MAY
Book & Chapter

1 Psalms 40, 41, 53,
55
2 Psalms, 58, 61, 62,
68
3 Psalms 72, 86, 101,
103
4 Psalms 108–110
5 Psalms 138–141
6 Psalms 143–145
7 1 Kings 1–4
8 Prov. 1–3
9 Prov. 4–6
10 Prov. 7–9
11 Prov. 10–12
12 Prov. 13–15
13 Prov. 16–18
14 Prov. 19–21
15 Prov. 22–24
16 Prov. 25–27

17 Prov. 28–31
18 S. of Sol. 1–4
19 S. of Sol. 5–8
20 1 Kings 5–7
21 1 Kings 8–11
22 Eccl. 1–3
23 Eccl. 4–6
24 Eccl. 7–9
25 Eccl. 10–12
26 1 Kings 12–14
27 1 Kings 15–17
28 1 Kings 18–20
29 1 Kings 21, 22; 2
Kings 1
30 2 Kings 2–4
31 2 Kings 5–7

JUNE
Book & Chapter

1 2 Kings 8–10
2 2 Kings 11–14:25
3 Jonah 1–4
4 2 Kings 14:26–29;
Amos 1–3
5 Amos 4–6
6 Amos 7–9
7 2 Kings 15–17
8 2 Kings 18–21
9 2 Kings 22–25
10 Psalms 1, 2, 10, 33
11 Psalms 43, 66, 67,
71
12 Psalms 89, 92, 93
13 Psalms 94–98
14 Psalms 99, 100, 102
15 Psalms 104, 106
16 Psalms 111–117
17 Psalms 118–119
18 Psalms 120–125
19 Psalms 127–133
20 Psalms 134–136
21 Psalms 146–150

22 1 Chron. 1–3
23 1 Chron. 4–6
24 1 Chron. 7–9
25 1 Chron. 10–12
26 1 Chron. 13–16
27 Psalms 42, 44, 45
28 Psalms 46–50
29 Psalms 73–76
30 Psalms 77–79

JULY
Book & Chapter

1 Psalms 80–83
2 Psalms 84, 85, 87, 88
3 1 Chron. 17–19
4 1 Chron. 20–22
5 1 Chron. 23–25
6 1 Chron. 26–29
7 2 Chron. 1–3
8 2 Chron. 4–6
9 2 Chron. 7–9
10 2 Chron. 10–12
11 2 Chron. 13–15
12 2 Chron. 16–18
13 2 Chron. 19–22
14 Joel 1–3; Obadiah
15 2 Chron. 23:1–26:8
16 Isaiah 1–3
17 Isaiah 4–6; 2 Chron. 26:9–23
18 2 Chron. 27–29
19 2 Chron. 30–32
20 Isaiah 7–9
21 Isaiah 10–12
22 Isaiah 13–15
23 Isaiah 16–18
24 Isaiah 19–21
25 Isaiah 22–24
26 Isaiah 25–27
27 Isaiah 28–30
28 Isaiah 31–33

29 Isaiah 34–36
30 Isaiah 37–39
31 Isaiah 40–42

AUGUST
Book & Chapter

1 Isaiah 43–45
2 Isaiah 46–48
3 Isaiah 49–51
4 Isaiah 52–54
5 Isaiah 55–57
6 Isaiah 58–60
7 Isaiah 61–63
8 Isaiah 64–66
9 Hosea 1–3
10 Hosea 4–6
11 Hosea 7–9
12 Hosea 10–12
13 Hosea 13, 14; Micah 1
14 Micah 2–4
15 Micah 5–7
16 Nahum 1–3
17 2 Chron. 33, 34; Zeph. 1
18 Zeph. 2, 3; 2 Chron. 35
19 Hab. 1–3
20 Jer. 1–3
21 Jer. 4–6
22 Jer. 11, 12, 26
23 Jer. 7–9
24 Jer. 10, 14, 15
25 Jer. 16–18
26 Jer. 19, 20, 35
27 Jer. 36, 45, 25
28 Jer. 46–49
29 Jer. 13, 22, 23
30 Jer. 24, 27, 28
31 Jer. 29, 50, 51

SEPTEMBER
Book & Chapter

1 Jer. 30–33
2 Jer. 21, 34, 37
3 Jer. 38, 39, 52
4 Jer. 40–42
5 Jer. 43, 44; Lam. 1
6 Lam. 2–5
7 2 Chron. 36:1–8; Daniel 1–3
8 Daniel 4–6
9 Daniel 7–9
10 Daniel 10–12
11 2 Chron. 36:9–21; Psalm 137
12 Ezekiel 1–4
13 Ezekiel 5–8
14 Ezekiel 9–12
15 Ezekiel 13–16
16 Ezekiel 17–20
17 Ezekiel 21–24
18 Ezekiel 25–28
19 Ezekiel 29–32
20 Ezekiel 33–36
21 Ezekiel 37–40
22 Ezekiel 41–44
23 Ezekiel 45–48
24 2 Chron. 36:22–23; Ezra 1–3
25 Ezra 4; Haggai 1, 2
26 Zech. 1–3
27 Zech. 4–6
28 Zech. 7–9
29 Zech. 10–12
30 Zech. 13, 14; Psalms 107, 126

OCTOBER
Book & Chapter

1 Ezra 5–7
2 Ezra 8–10

3 Esther 1–3
4 Esther 4–6
5 Esther 7–10
6 Neh. 1–3
7 Neh. 4–6
8 Neh. 7–9
9 Neh. 10–13
10 Malachi 1–4
11 Matthew 1–3
12 Matthew 4–7
13 Matthew 8–10
14 Matthew 11–13
15 Matthew 14–16
16 Matthew 17–19
17 Matthew 20–22
18 Matthew 23–25
19 Matthew 26–28
20 Mark 1–3
21 Mark 4–6
22 Mark 7–9
23 Mark 10–12
24 Mark 13–16
25 Luke 1, 2
26 Luke 3–5
27 Luke 6–8
28 Luke 9–11
29 Luke 12–14
30 Luke 15–17
31 Luke 18–20

NOVEMBER
Book & Chapter

1 Luke 21–24
2 John 1,2
3 John 3–5
4 John 6–8
5 John 9–11
6 John 12–14
7 John 15–17
8 John 18–21
9 Acts 1–4
10 Acts 5:1—8:3

11 Acts 8:4—11:18
12 Acts 11:19—14:28
13 James 1:1—3:12
14 James 3:13—5:20; Acts 15
15 Gal. 1–3
16 Gal. 4–6
17 Acts 16; Phil. 1, 2
18 Phil. 3, 4; Acts 17:1–10
19 1 Thess. 1–3
20 1 Thess. 4, 5
21 2 Thess. 1–3; Acts 17:11—18:11
22 1 Cor. 1–3
23 1 Cor. 4–7
24 1 Cor. 8:1—11:1
25 1 Cor. 11:2—14:40
26 1 Cor. 15, 16
27 2 Cor. 1–3
28 2 Cor. 4–6
29 2 Cor. 7–9
30 2 Cor. 10–13

DECEMBER
Book & Chapter

1 Acts 18:12—19:41; Eph. 1–3
2 Eph. 4–6
3 Romans 1–3
4 Romans 4–6
5 Romans 7–9
6 Romans 10–12
7 Romans 13–16
8 Acts 20:1—23:11
9 Acts 23:12—26:32
10 Acts 27, 28, Col. 1
11 Col. 2–4
12 Heb. 1–3
13 Heb. 4–6
14 Heb. 7–9
15 Heb. 10–13; Titus

16 Philemon; 1 Tim. 1–3
17 1 Tim. 4–6
18 2 Tim. 1–3
19 2 Tim. 4; 1 Peter 1, 2
20 1 Peter 3–5
21 2 Peter 1–3
22 1 John 1–3
23 1 John 4, 5; 2 John
24 3 John; Jude; Rev. 1
25 Rev. 2–4
26 Rev. 5—8:5
27 Rev. 8:6—11:19
28 Rev. 12, 13
29 Rev. 14–16
30 Rev. 17–19
31 Rev. 20–22

[1]Basic outline by Stanley M. Horton: Courtesy, Gospel Publishing House; and reprinted here by permission of the National Association of Evangelicals.